The Fundamentals of Creative Design
Gavin Ambrose/Paul Harris

academia

An AVA Book

Published by AVA Publishing SA
Rue des Fontenailles 16
Case Postale
1000 Lausanne 6
Switzerland
Tel: +41 786 005 109
Email: enquiries@avabooks.com

Distributed by Thames & Hudson (ex-North America)
181a High Holborn
London WC1V 7QX
United Kingdom
Tel: +44 20 7845 5000
Fax: +44 20 7845 5055
Email: sales@thameshudson.co.uk
www.thamesandhudson.com

Distributed in the USA & Canada by:
Ingram Publisher Services Inc.
1 Ingram Blvd.
La Vergne TN 37086
USA
Tel: +1 866 400 5351
Fax: +1 800 838 1149
Email: customer.service@ingrampublisherservices.com

English Language Support Office
AVA Publishing (UK) Ltd.
Tel: +44 1903 204 455
Email: enquiries@avabooks.com

Second edition © AVA Publishing SA 2011
First published in 2003

ISBN 978-2-940411-61-0

Library of Congress Cataloging-in-Publication Data
Ambrose, Gavin; Harris, Paul.
The Fundamentals of Creative Design / Gavin Ambrose, Paul Harris p.cm.
Includes bibliographical references and index.
ISBN: 9782940411610 (pbk.:alk.paper)
eISBN: 9782940447251
1.Graphic design (Typography).2.Graphic arts.
NC997 .A43 2011

10 9 8 7 6 5 4 3 2 1

Design by Gavin Ambrose

Production by AVA Book Production Pte. Ltd., Singapore
Tel: +65 6334 8173
Fax: +65 6259 9830
Email: production@avabooks.com.sg

Gavin Ambrose/Paul Harris

2nd
edition

The Fundamentals
of Creative Design

Ethical: aware-
ness/
reflect-
ion/
debate

ava
academia

contents

92 Image

A potent communication tool that can bring a design to life and convey ideas to a reader in a way that text alone cannot. Images explain design and also add drama and meaning.

116 Colour

Creatively used, colour can increase the visual appeal of a design and enhance message communication. Understanding the principles of colour equips a designer to reliably control its usage and maximize its impact.

144 Print finishing

Various techniques can add a finishing touch to a print job to help differentiate it and give it something extra – both visually and functionally.

The Modern Poster

A REVIEW OF CONTEMPORARY POSTER DESIGN BY MICHAEL JOHNSON, JOHNSON BANKS

Introduction

IT HAS BEEN ALMOST A DECADE SINCE THE FIRST EDITION OF THE FUNDAMENTALS OF CREATIVE DESIGN WAS FIRST PUBLISHED. THIS SECOND EDITION IS INTENDED AS A GUIDE TO EQUIP BOTH STUDENTS AND PRACTITIONERS ENGAGED IN DESIGN WITH THE LONG-ESTABLISHED TENETS THAT UNDERPIN BOTH PRINT AND DIGITAL ASPECTS OF THE DISCIPLINE.

THIS NEW EDITION RETAINS THE VIBRANCY OF THE FIRST, BUT IT HAS BEEN IMPROVED, REFRESHED AND RE-STRUCTURED TO CONVEY ITS LESSONS AND MESSAGES IN AN EVEN MORE ACCESSIBLE MANNER. THIS UPDATED VOLUME CONTAINS NEW CHAPTERS, NEW CREATIVE EXAMPLES AND STUDENT EXERCISES TO PROVIDE CONCISE, ILLUSTRATED EXPLANATIONS OF THE DESIGN FUNDAMENTALS AND EXAMPLES OF THEIR PRACTICAL APPLICATION USING CONTEMPORARY DESIGN PROJECTS.

THE SECOND EDITION OF THE FUNDAMENTALS OF CREATIVE DESIGN OFFERS A UNIQUE RESOURCE TO ALL DESIGN PRACTITIONERS, STUDENTS AND MEMBERS OF THE GENERAL PUBLIC WITH AN INTEREST IN DESIGN.

The Modern Poster ←

The Johnson Banks studio took a tongue-in-cheek approach for the poster on the left to promote a review of contemporary poster design by creating a clean minimalist image that looks as though it is constructed of four separate posters. It gives the impression of a billboard that has somehow fallen out of alignment.

Design: Johnson Banks

THERE'S NOT MUCH DIFFERENCE BETWEEN ADVERTISING AND DESIGN. A TALK BY MICHAEL JOHNSON, JOHNSON BANKS

Format

Format is the physical shape and size of a final product whether it be a book, magazine, brochure, a piece of packaging or even a website. Format selection is a combination of the designer's vision and practical considerations. These considerations may include who the target audience is, where the design will be viewed or used, the nature of the information to be presented and the budget available.

A creative approach to format selection can produce dramatic results that enhance the overall message being presented. Format selection includes materials, the scale of production and the use of print finishing techniques, all of which can enhance a design and result in something unique without necessarily exceeding a budget.

Advertising and design   ←

The poster format gives designers a great deal of space – but this doesn't mean a design has to be complicated. Often, the most successful designs are simple solutions writ large. This poster plays with the linguistic similarities between 'advertising' and 'design' – the two words are overlaid to confirm how similar the two disciplines really are. A literal 'two-in-one' – the poster says both advertising and design, and makes a statement about both.

Design: Johnson Banks

choosing a page size

Theoretically, a designer can use whatever page size they prefer, but the visual impact must be taken into consideration. A theory that divides and defines the space on a page has been developed so that a page is logical, easy to work with and, most importantly, gives proportions that are easy on the eye. Having a variety of page sizes with appealing proportions saves the designer time and provides a sound starting point for any design.

Page size

Although a designer is free to choose any page size there are practical and economic considerations that will influence that choice, such as paper wastage and the cost of cutting non-standard sizes. The existence of ISO (International Organization for Standardization) paper sizes provides a range of paper sizes that may seem unadventurous, but nevertheless works and is freely available.

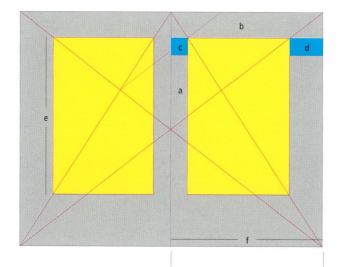

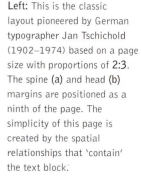

Left: This is the classic layout pioneered by German typographer Jan Tschichold (1902–1974) based on a page size with proportions of **2:3**. The spine (**a**) and head (**b**) margins are positioned as a ninth of the page. The simplicity of this page is created by the spatial relationships that 'contain' the text block.

The grid creates harmonious proportions: the inner margin (**c**) is half the size of the outer margin (**d**), while the height of the text block (**e**) is equal to the width of the page (**f**).

Jan Tschichold left Germany in 1933 and worked in Switzerland as a typographer until 1946. Between 1946 and 1949, he lived and worked in England overseeing the typographic redesign of the fast expanding publisher, Penguin Books.

Layout developments

For over a thousand years page sizes have been constructed using pentagons, hexagons, octagons, circles, squares and triangles. Early scribes and typographers, influenced by organic phenomena, such as the hexagonal construction of honeycomb and the pentagonal structures found in the growth of flowers, used these shapes as the basis for page sizes. In turn, became were the basis for determining the active area on the page within which the text and graphics will be positioned.

1 – Tall pentagon layout

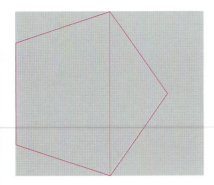 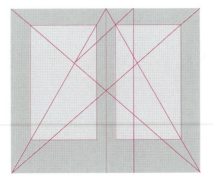 

Above: The tall pentagon page is constructed by vertically dissecting a rotated pentagon. This gives a page size that creates a double-page spread when doubled.

Above: The double-page spread is then dissected from bottom left to top right, bottom right to top left, bottom left to top centre and bottom right to top centre. The header and spine widths are then inserted to complete the necessary anchor points for the text block. These are usually based on a division of the height (i.e. a twelfth).

Above: The resulting layout gives a basic indication of the position for the main body copy or text block.

This process can be repeated to create different page formats using different areas of the same pentagon (see below).

2 – Truncated pentagon layout

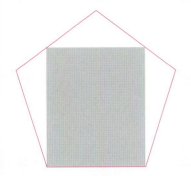 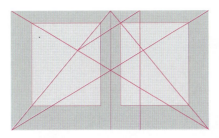 

3 – Short pentagon layout

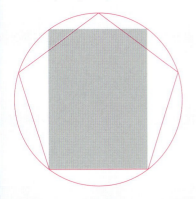 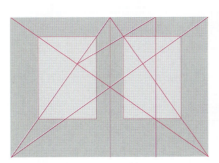 

Standard book sizes

The size of a book is determined by two main factors: the size of the original sheet of paper that the pages are made from, and the number of times that sheet of paper is folded before it is trimmed. A sheet of paper is typically folded several times to form a section or signature and many sections are bound together to form a book. **Folio editions** are books made of signatures that have been folded only once. **Quarto editions** are formed from twice folded signatures (making four leaves or eight pages), and **Octavo editions** are bound from signatures folded three times (making eight leaves or 16 pages). The format used for a job is partly determined by pragmatism – an atlas, for example, tends to be large and a novel small – but also on proportion, and how the publication will feel to hold. The illustration below shows the different proportions of the sizes shown in the table on the right.

Non-standard sizes

Designers often use standard sizes, but non-standard sizes are also available. Non-standard sizes can be obtained by manipulating a standard size (by cutting away its top or side for example) to create a new non-standard shape.

Paper size bound book sizes as follows:	mm x mm
Demy 16mo	143mm x 111mm
Demy 18mo	146mm x 95mm
Foolscap Octavo (8vo)	171mm x 108mm
Crown (8vo)	191mm x 127mm
Large Crown 8vo	203mm x 133mm
Demy 8vo	222mm x 143mm
Medium 8vo	241mm x 152mm
Royal 8vo	254mm x 159mm
Super Royal 8vo	260mm x 175mm
Imperial 8vo	279mm x 191mm
Foolscap Quarto (4to)	216mm x 171mm
Crown 4to	254mm x 191mm
Demy 4to	260mm x 222mm
Royal 4to	318mm x 254mm
Imperial 4to	381mm x 279mm
Crown Folio	381mm x 254mm
Demy Folio	445mm x 286mm
Royal Folio	508mm x 318mm
Music	356mm x 260mm

Above: Different page sizes have different proportions. This relationship of height to width has as big an impact on a page layout as the basic size of the book.

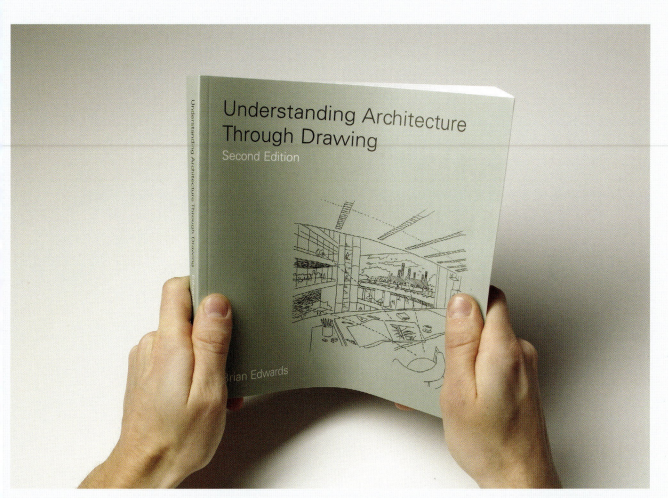

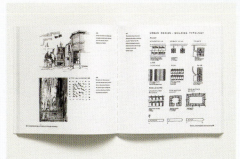 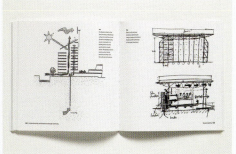

**Understanding Architecture
Through Drawing** ↑ ←

This non-standard format
is 21.8cm x 21.6cm, an
amended Demy 4to. This
format was selected as it
'lent' itself to the format
of the content, shown left.

Design: Gavin Ambrose

I am the Devil when I'm here;
I am God when I'm outside.

Cuando estoy aquí, soy el Diablo;
cuando estoy en el exterior, soy Dios.

I HAVE
NO FEAR
OF DEATH
AT ALL,
I HAVE
ALREADY
DIED TWICE

ICH HABE
KEINE ANGST
VOR DEM
TOD, ICH
BIN SCHON
ZWEIMAL
GESTORBEN

Benetton ↑ ← ↓

The examples on this spread were taken from the bi-monthly Colors magazine sponsored by Benetton. The spacious pages of the magazine lend themselves well to displaying full-bleed photography. The magazine is also produced with two covers: one global and one local. It is published in seven languages.

Design: Pentagram

ISO and American paper sizes

Standard paper sizes provide a convenient and efficient means for designers, printers and others involved in printing and publishing to communicate product specifications and keep costs down. Standardized paper sizes can be traced back to 14th-century Bologna in Italy where the outlines for four paper sizes were given to guide local paper manufacturers.

The modern ISO (International Organization for Standardization) paper sizes system is based on an observation by the German physics professor Georg Christoph Lichtenberg, who in 1786 saw the advantages of paper sizes having a height-to-width ratio of the square root of two (1:1.4142). Paper using this Lichtenberg ratio will maintain its aspect ratio when cut in half.

You can see this principle quite clearly by performing a simple experiment. Take a sheet of A4 paper. This has a size of 297 x 210mm, and a ratio of 1:161803. If you fold this in half, and then rotate the page by 90°, you have the next size in the sequence, in this case A5. The size is different, but one measurement remains the same – the height of A5 is equal to the width of A4 – 210mm. Although the page size is smaller, the ratio of height to width is the same, as shown below.

France was the first country to adopt paper sizes equivalent to modern ISO sizes with a law issued in 1794. Today, Canada and the USA are the only industrialized countries that do not use the ISO system.

The ISO sizes are based on the metric system using the square-root-of-two ratio with format A0 having an area of one square metre. As this does not allow the page height and width to be rounded metric lengths the area of the page has been defined to have a round metric value, which simplifies the calculation of the weight of a document (format x number of pages) as paper is usually specified in g/m^2.

The A series comprises a range of paper sizes that differs from the next size by a factor of either 2 or $1/2$. B series sizes are intermediate sizes and C series sizes are for envelopes that can contain A size stationery. RA and SRA stock sizes are sheets of paper from which A sizes can be cut.

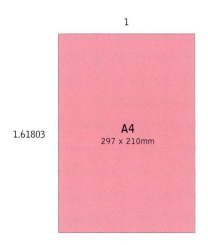

1

1.61803

A4
297 x 210mm

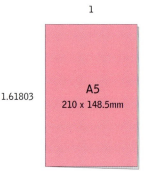

1

1.61803

A5
210 x 148.5mm

Take a sheet of paper in the A series of sizes...

Fold it in half across its width and rotate 90°...

It is now half the size, but with the same ratio of height to width.

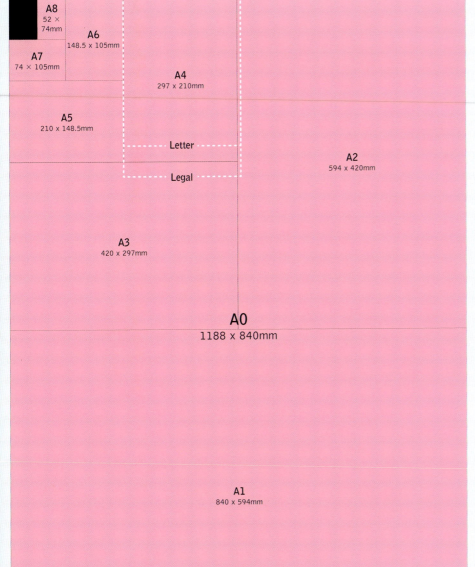

A8
52 ×
74mm

A6
148.5 x 105mm

A7
74 × 105mm

A4
297 x 210mm

A5
210 x 148.5mm

Letter

Legal

A2
594 x 420mm

A3
420 x 297mm

A0
1188 x 840mm

A1
840 x 594mm

ISO A Sizes

Shown below are the main A sizes in the ISO system. These were calculated using millimetres.

	mm x mm
A0	841 × 1189
A1	594 × 841
A2	420 × 594
A3	297 × 420
A4	210 × 297
A5	148 × 210
A6	105 × 148
A7	74 × 105
A8	52 × 74
A9	37 × 52
A10	26 × 37

North American paper sizes

Shown below are the main US paper sizes. These were calculated using inches.

	in x in	mm x mm
Letter	8.5 × 11	216 × 279
Legal	8.5 × 14	216 × 356
Ledger	17 × 11	432 × 279
Tabloid	11 × 17	279 × 432

PA4-based series

Shown below are the PA series, sometimes used in Canada. These were calculated using inches and a logical aspect ratio.

	mm x mm	ratio
PA0	840 × 1120	3:4
PA1	560 × 840	2:3
PA2	420 × 560	3:4
PA3	280 × 420	2:3
PA4	210 × 280	3:4

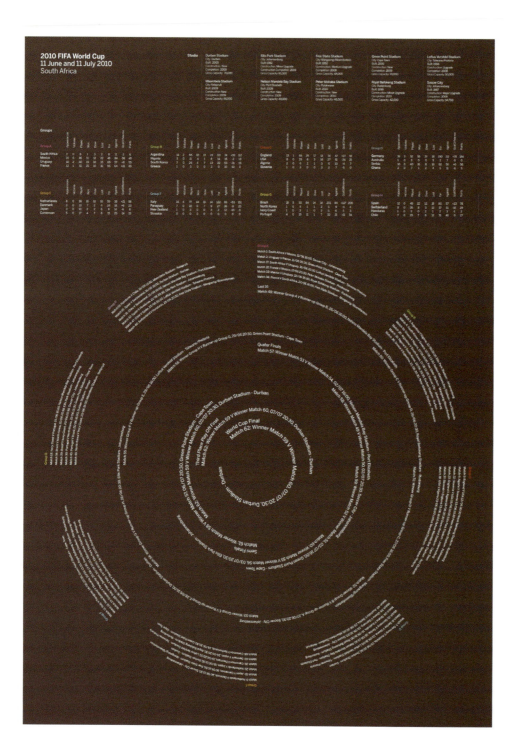

FIFA ← ↑

This typographic diary of
football fixtures and dates
exploits the space afforded
by an A1 poster format.
Design: Planning Unit

Matchroom stadium →

This series of posters of
famous football stadia are
available in either A2, A1 or
A0. The abstraction of shape
and form creates a series of
graphic shapes, with location
information appearing in the
bottom left-hand corner. As
the proportions of the three
sizes are the same, the posters
can be scaled up without
altering their proportions.
Design: Jeff Knowles

HORNSEY ROAD
DRAYTON PARK
QUEENSLAND ROAD
BRYANTWOOD ROAD

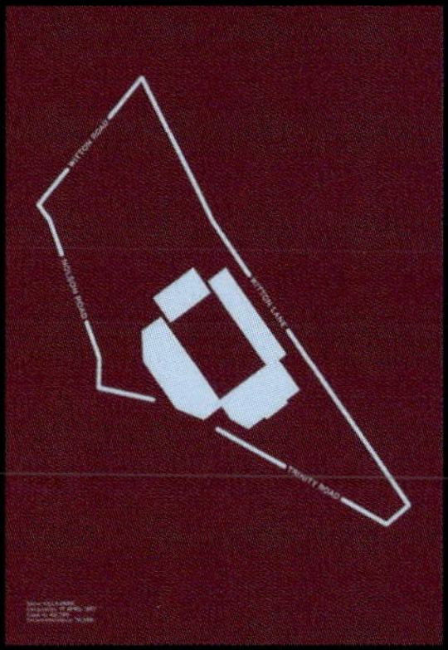
WITTON ROAD
WITTON LANE
TRINITY ROAD

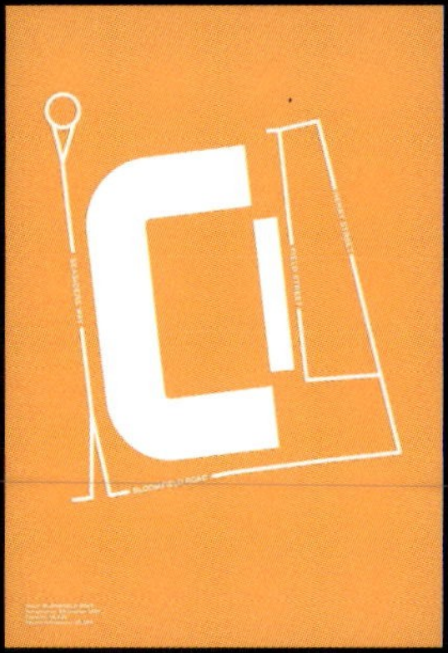

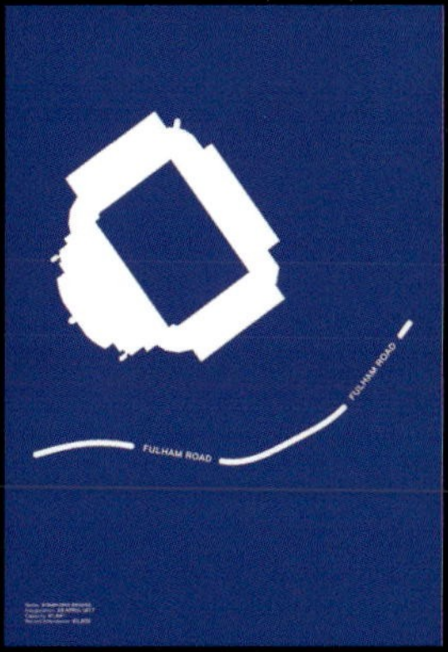
FULHAM ROAD
FULHAM ROAD

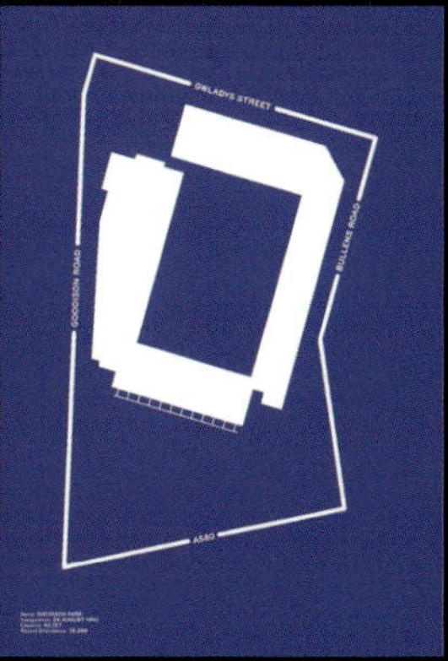
GWLADYS STREET
GOODISON ROAD
BULLENS ROAD
A580

ASHTON NEW ROAD

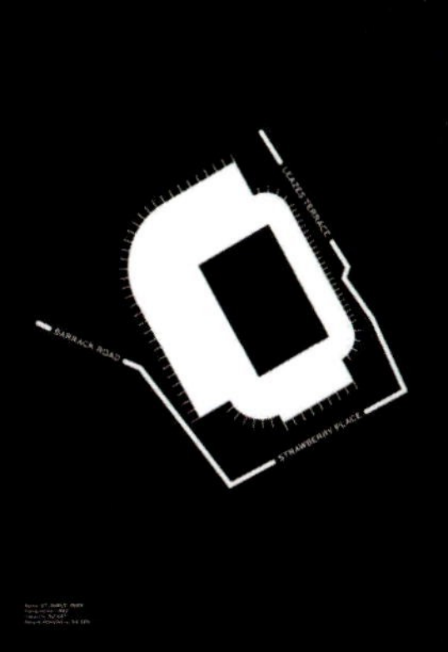
LEAZES TERRACE
BARRACK ROAD
STRAWBERRY PLACE

STANLEY MATTHEWS WAY

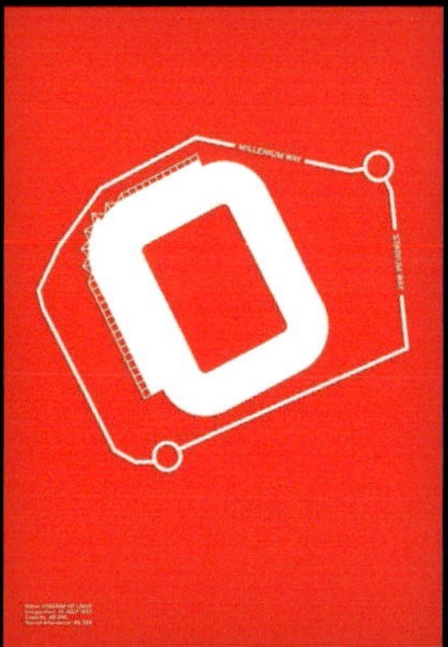
MILLENNIUM WAY

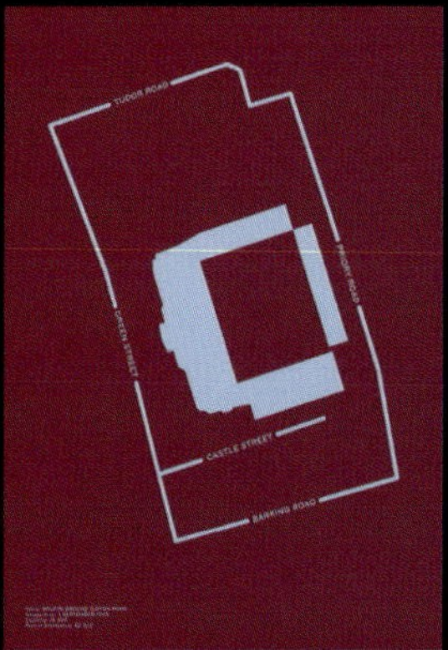
TUDOR ROAD
CASTLE STREET
BARKING ROAD

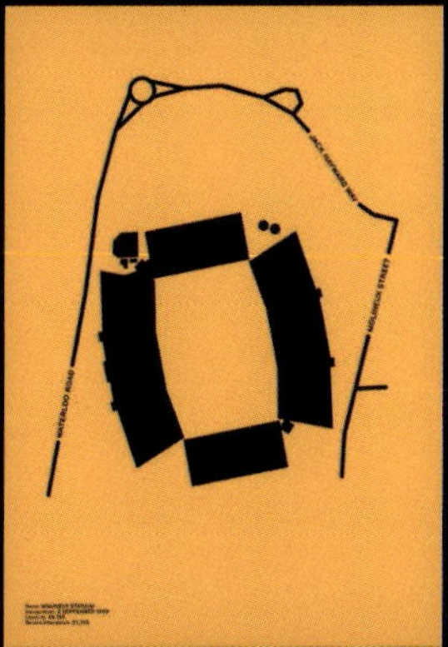
WATERLOO ROAD
MOLINEUX STREET

Merchant ↓ ↘ →

In this annual report by Merchant, standardization is forsaken
resulting in an unusual and engaging mixture of formats.
Compartmentalized segments of information are allocated
individual page sizes that become surprisingly easy to navigate.
High-gloss inner sections contrast with the cool hues of the
introduction, bringing an element of surprise and a change of pace.

Design: NB: Studio

Below: A selection of page
sizes are used for the series
of small vignette brochures
contained in the overall
document. This creates a
'tabbed' index system that
allows for ease of use, while
also adding graphic impact.

The view from the US.

From good to great in a few letters.

Reporting from the EU.

'The question
we are asking is
whether you can
trust the numbers
you have received
from companies.'

Fund Manager

'A combination
of seeing
management and
reading their
commentary in
the annual report
gives you a more
visceral sense of
management
competence and
sense of purpose
looking forward.
You don't get this
by reading the
notes on the
treatment of a
Venezuelan tax
charge.'

Fund Manager

Corporate
social
responsibility.
3 different angles.

XBRL
1. An architect.
2. A stakeholder.
3. A user.

Merchant

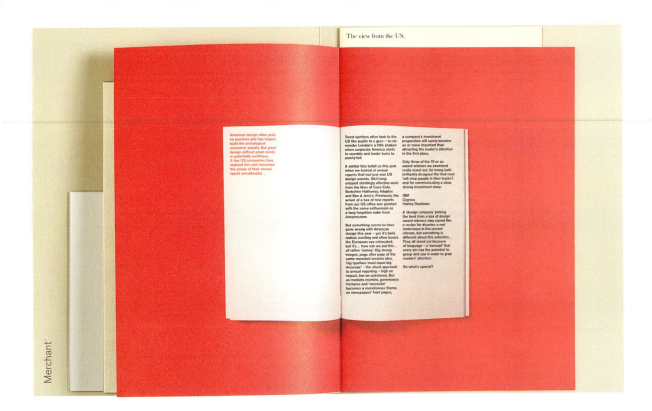

Above: Although most of the changes in paper size are actual, that is to say they are physically different-sized pieces of paper, this is not the case for all. Shown above is a spread where the smaller page size is printed – a form of trompe l'oeil – where the eye is tricked into seeing something that isn't there.

Right: The bold confident use of flat 'flood' colour creates visual punctuation to the document's pace.

standard web sizes

Designing work that will be viewed on a screen or monitor presents some different considerations from designing for print. The main consideration is the physical distance that people will view the design from. However, one can utilize various format aspects in the virtual world that are unavailable to physical print media.

Web page formats are not restricted by the physical extent and dimensions of a book or magazine, as a designer can harness the unlimited virtual space available with devices such as pop-up boxes, animations, pull-down menus, rollovers and navigation bars. However, there is a danger of creating a design overloaded with devices, which could crowd and confuse.

A computer or TV screen has a limited number of pixels that can be viewed at one time. However, because elements such as menus and scroll bars take up space, the live space is not always as big as the screen pixel dimensions. The common screen resolutions typically used for the presentation of websites are SVGA 800x600 and XGA 1024x768.

Fixed vs scrolling
Websites can have fixed or scrolling pages and this really depends on how you would like to deliver the content. If content can be placed on one page, web browsers can show it without scrolling. More complex information delivery may need to have content that falls below the visible screen. In this case, the content has an electronic 'fold'. The electronic 'fold' is the point at which the content disappears from view at the bottom of the screen. Typically, the most important information appears above the fold and secondary information is positioned below it.

Liquid layout
Web and digital media designers can use liquid layouts that stretch to fill whatever screen size the viewer wants to view them on, rather than being a fixed size. This offers versatility and means the viewer does not have to alter their viewing preferences to comfortably see the content.

Pixels
The individual pieces of colour information that comprise a screen.

Resolution
The total number of vertical x horizontal pixels.

Scroll bars
Vertical and horizontal bars used to move up or down a page.

The fold
The bottom of the visible screen page. Content below the fold should generally be considered secondary to the content above. Crucial content, such as contact details, should, where possible, be above the fold.

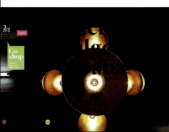

2nd Floor   ←   ↑

These images are from a website created for a leading Greek designer store. The home page features several rotating flood images in the background (middle) over which a scrolling menu 'floats' to lead viewers to the product pages (bottom left).

Design: Beetroot

film and moving image

Technological advances mean that we are exposed to and use an increasing array of devices that support moving images and can display an increasing range of colours at increasing resolutions. Even relatively basic display panels now have strong and varied capabilities. Designers are increasingly tasked with providing moving imagery for websites, films, television, DVDs or online advertising. Graphic content in TV began to increase with the mounting popularity of MTV in the 1980s; this was characterized by the repeated use of innovative and creative station idents and other on-screen graphic elements in addition to moving pictures. Designers also enhance film sequences in post production by using overlaid type and illustration to catch the attention of the viewer and convey key messages.

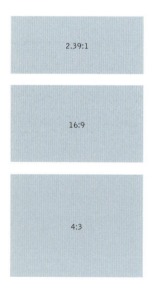

Film is available in different formats. The format typically used depends upon where the film will ultimately be shown or used. A film shot for cinema release is one of the wider formats – either 2.39:1 or 1.85:1. Film is then re-edited for use on television, where the standard format is 16:9. Older TVs and computer monitors may use a format of 4:3. Material filmed on the wider formats can be played at narrower aspect ratios, which is achieved by cropping, zooming or letterboxing. Letterboxing adds horizontal mattes to the top and bottom sections of a film to preserve the original aspect ratio. Three commonly used aspect ratios used in film and television are shown on the left. The top, 2.39:1, is a cinema or theatre format; 16:9 is a widescreen format and 4:3 is a TV format. With each format, the perimeter needs to be avoided when placing or using text. Avoiding the 10% strip around the edges is deemed the safe zone, as shown below.

Below are three types of safe zone: letterboxing, windowboxing and pillar boxing.

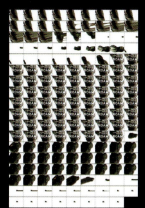

Minority Report ↑

These images are pre-vision sequences for the feature film Minority Report. Each is a foreshadowing of a murder to come and all were pivotal moments in the film. The sequences combined special camera work, editing and designing s that each element worked in harmony to add to the compelling story.

Design: ImaginaryForces / Matt Checkowski

Transitions ←   ↙

Image manipulation is not restricted to static images. In the sequence on the left and below, the shape of a shoe is changed by breaking the image down into vertical lines that then gradually disappear before reforming as a watch.

Design: ImaginaryForces / Matt Checkowski

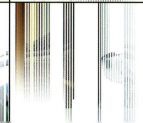

AIR PRESTO
ROAM
(WATERPROOF

AIR PRES

Portland Trail Blazers ↑

The above images are from a broadcast and stadium screen identity for the NBA basketball team, the Portland Trail Blazers. They captured the emotion the team brings to the game within a framework that unified the franchise brand. The design has iconic red, black and silver graphic stripes that seem to have a life of their own. The design jumps off the players' uniforms and forms logos, transitions, crowd prompts and team match-up screens. All elements move dynamically and lead to an identity that literally bounces to the beat of the basketball and shuffles to the movement of the players.

Design: ImaginaryForces/Matt Checkowski

Deployment of film onto web

When use of the World Wide Web first became widespread, slow download speeds meant that film could not be effectively embedded and used in this medium. As technology has improved, so has the performance power of personal computers; this also led to improved download speeds, which means it is now possible to include film clips on web pages and view streaming content such as sporting events, TV shows and films online. With this change in user habits, film elements (or assets) are increasingly deployed into web spaces to create a more fluid, immersive environment. Adding the dynamism of film to the web results in a viewing experience increasingly controlled on demand by the user.

Eric Parry Architects ↙ ↓

This website for Eric Parry Architects is almost devoid of navigation, with only a simple 'node-and-line' bar at the base of the movie. This bar is reminiscent of the underground map, implying that the user can move through the films and, indeed, through London. Mark Logue's films are given centre stage and prominence with all other elements 'fading' into the background.

Design: Urbik / Mark Logue / Gavin Ambrose

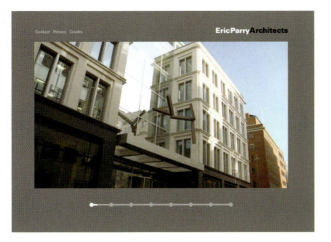

File types

MPEG (.MPG)

The Moving Pictures Expert Group (MPEG) format is a final product video format originally developed for low bit-rate video communications, but its usage and scope has expanded due to its efficiency across a wide range of bit-rates up to tens of megabits per second. MPEG files are compressed films that contain both audio and video, and maintain most of the original film quality, hence its popularity for encoding film trailers and music videos on the web.

AVI (.AVI)

AVI or Audio Video Interleave was introduced by Microsoft in 1992 to put video into Windows. AVI is a container file that contains audio and video, and allows synchronous audio/video playback. AVI supports multiple streaming audio and video. Designers often use the AVI format for editing the video content and then encode the final product in MPEG. AVI can result in large file sizes when low compression rates are used.

Flash Video (.FLV)

Flash Video is a file format that delivers video over the internet using Adobe Flash Player. Flash is the format of choice for embedding video on the web, as virtually everyone has Adobe Flash Player installed in their web browser. Also, most video sharing websites stream video in Flash, including YouTube and the BBC. The Flash format also yields one of the smallest file sizes after compression and retains reasonable quality.

file formats

Various file formats are available to a designer for storing images, each of which offers particular benefits and drawbacks. File formats include TIFF, JPEG, PSD, PDF, EPS and BITMAP. These file formats essentially represent the work flow of the graphic design process and the different files used as a job progresses.

Looking at images

An image contains information. When viewed in an image manipulation program, the top of the image shows its file name (A), file format (B), its colour mode (C), and its bit depth (D). In the example below, these last two are CMYK and 8 bits. Being familiar with these variables is important when it comes to saving and storing images. It is normal for an image to be an eight-bit file, though original images captured professionally are often 16- or even 32-bit files. The higher bit files are normally used when working on an image, before saving it down to a more manageable file size.

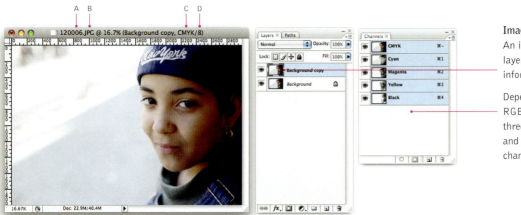

Image facets

An image can have multiple layers that contain different information and treatments.

Depending on whether it is RGB or CMYK it will have three of four colour channels, and an additional composite channel.

Saving images

As various file formats are available when saving an image, the main consideration is what it is being saved for. If an image is to be used for print, then generally it will be saved as a TIFF in CMYK format at 300 dpi. If an image is to be used on screen, it will generally be saved as a JPEG in RGB at a resolution of either 96 or 72 dpi.

Compression

Images can be compressed (A) to create a file with a smaller file size. File size is reduced by limiting the amount of information contained in an image, which means that image quality is lowered. When compressing images, there is a balance of quality over file size. For screen use, a 96-dpi image will look the same as a 300-dpi image as they are both viewed on a monitor. However, 300-dpi images will take longer to load as they have bigger file sizes. Loading speed is one of the reasons that lower resolutions are preferred for screen usage.

Layers

When working on an image with different layers, it needs to be saved as a PSD, TIFF, or Large Document Format file with layers, otherwise it will be flattened into a single image that you will not be able to edit.

The images below show different file formats using the same image for comparison.

RGB and CMYK
Images that use either three- or four-channel colour. RGB results in smaller file sizes than CMYK, but CMYK is needed for four-colour printing.

GIF
A file format for compressing line and flat colour images that are to be used for web applications. These images become smaller as less colours are used (eight colours are used in this example).

Greyscale
A continuous tone produced from grey tones.

TIFF
Saving a greyscale image as a TIFF allows it to be coloured in an image-manipulation program.

Bitmap
A raster image composed of pixels in a grid at a fixed resolution. There are different patterns and levels available when making a bitmap.

JPEG
JPEG files can be compressed to reduced file size, but image quality degrades if compressed too far, as shown here.

Duotone
This was saved in EPS format, and contains two colours – yellow and black. Tritones and quadtones contain three and four colours respectively. They can also be 'flooded,' where the background is 100% of the colour, as shown here.

EPS
EPS files are also used for saving duotones, but they are primarily used for saving vector images, such as illustrations and logotypes.

Format / Proportion

Exercise #1 – Format

Premise
Numerous format choices are available to present information in different ways.

Exercise
Imagine you have three different clients – each wanting an innovative, eye-catching design that highlights key information. Think about what formats (including different sizes, materials and folding methods) can be used to produce a gallery auction catalogue, a music company brochure and a transport map. Don't be restricted by what you think this format 'should' be.

Outcome
Produce a visualization of your solutions explaining the choices you have made and how they meet the needs of the different clients.

Aim
To encourage a more considered appreciation of the use of format in design and where the use of format techniques can produce notable results.

Medway map ← ↑

This poster by Urbik features a series of folds that reveal information. The map is a combination of the real, what is already in the Medway area, and a map of ideas and possibilities – the things that will be there in the future. This is a traditional format to use for a map, but how could the same information be contained in a book, a series of stamps or a pack of playing cards?

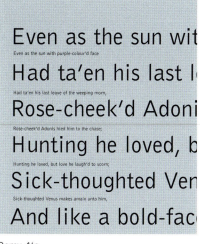

Demy 4to

Crown Folio

Medium 8vo

Exercise #2 – Proportion

Premise
The format used for a design changes its visual impact.

Exercise
Select a piece of text, such as a poem or a recipe, and set it on three different page sizes taken from page 12 of this chapter.

Outcome
Produce a visualization of your solutions and comment on how the proportions of different page sizes affect the design in terms of spacing, typesize used, typographic colour, overall visual impression etc.

Aim
To show how format selection can affect the tone and outcome of a design.

Proportion ↑

How does the proportion of a page affect or influence how you set text? Experimenting with a series of page sizes can produce dramatically different effects, from calm to active, and from dynamic to static.

The importance of being Dree

Dree Hemingway's wolfbury looks and tragedy tinged literary heritage have entranced the fashion world. Here, she hits the Hollywood hills to showcase Simone Rocha's sultry winter collection.

Belle heir

When your grandfather and aunt are Hollywood royalty, it's hard to break out on your own and make a name for yourself. Fortunately for Gia Coppola, her innate talent behind the lens is there for everyone to see, winning her praise and kudos for her powerful photography and attention-grabbing shorts.

Double vision

For over thirty years French artist Sophie Calle has worked quietly on the periphery of contemporary art. Armed with a unique blend of text and images, Calle explores the nature of human identity. Her approach is personal, provocative and innately feminine. She's even consulted a clairvoyant for her art - the spirit world's response: 'Go to hell.'

This year Calle is awarded one of photography's highest accolades - The Hasselblad International Award in Photography. To mark the occasion Twin talks to the artist's admirers, curators and collaborators to discover what makes her vision so unique.

Layout and grids

Layout is the arrangement of the design elements in relation to the space that they occupy as part of an overall design scheme. Layout can also be called the management of form and space. The objective of layout is to present the visual and textural elements that are to be communicated in a manner that enables the reader to receive them with the minimum of effort. With good layout, a reader can easily navigate through complex information in both print and electronic media.

The positioning of the various elements in a layout is guided by the use of a grid – a series of reference lines that help a designer divide and arrange a page to allow quick and accurate placement of design elements. Grids also ensure consistency from page to page.

TWIN ←

The beauty of a grid becomes apparent over a series of spreads. Some items remain constant, while others alter. Pace is added, type size varied, and the relationship of images altered, to create an engaging and dynamic design.

Design: Research Studios / Planning Unit

why use a grid?

This might seem like an odd question as we are taught in simple terms that a grid is needed; a grid is good. But what is it for? And is it always good? As a designer, you need to have an understanding of how to construct a grid, and of the different types of grids at your disposal.

Josef Müller-Brockman (1914–1996) established his own design practice in 1936 having been an apprentice in Zürich. He is often cited as an influence on modern design, particularly grid systems. On this page is a mantra devised by Müller-Brockman explaining the purpose of the grid. From this, it is clear that the grid offers two very different results: one logical and one emotional. Müller-Brockman first talks about the ability of the grid to objectively present an argument, and that the grid is systematical and logical. However, he also talks of rhythm and tension, terms we might associate more with art or poetry. This is the point of the grid: it should enable the designer to effectively create designs akin to works of art or poetry.

Different grids for different purposes

There is no absolute grid. There are in fact as many grids as designs. The grid developed for any particular job will vary and will often need to be adapted as the design develops. Over the following pages, we will explore some different approaches to how a designer can develop a grid. Ultimately, the grid should facilitate freedom of design rather than hinder it. It should make the placing of items easier and logical. What grid to use, or indeed, whether or not to use a grid, should be governed by the intent of the work. What are you trying to achieve? Is a grid going to help you achieve this?

Working with a grid / working without a grid

Working with a grid gives a designer an immediate structure to work with in order to guide design element placement, which contributes to an efficient and speedy design process. A grid also allows a designer to maintain design consistency over different pages or a series of publications. Working without a grid gives a designer total flexibility over the placement of design elements. However, the lack of structure means that all spatial relationships between objects will have to be thought about and determined. Potentially, this will increase the required design time and result in imprecise designs. Working without a grid also makes it more difficult to maintain design consistency over different pages.

a
to construct the argument objectively with the means of visual communication

b
to construct the text and illustrative material systematically and logically

c
to organize the text and illustrations in a compact arrangement with its own rhythm

d
to put together the visual material so that it is readily intelligible and structured with a high degree of tension

Josef Müller-Brockman, 1981

Metropolis   ←

The use of a curvaceous serif font for the article title contrasts well with the content of the article. The typographical presentation leads one to challenge normal perceptions of content presentation as does the use of an angled grid. The unusual angle leaves large areas of white space and reinforces the message that abstract design ideas can improve the world around us.

Design: Pentagram

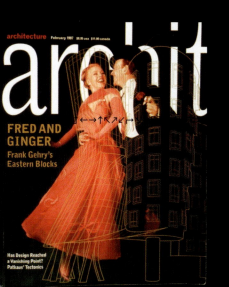

Architecture   ↑   ↖

The cover layout of Architecture magazine sees the masthead extend onto the contents page inside – an active approach that adds dynamism to the publication.

To me good design means as little design as possible.

Simple is better than complicated.

Quiet is better than loud.

Unobtrusive is better than exciting.

Small is better than large.

Light is better than heavy.

Plain is better than coloured.

Harmony is better than divergency.

Being well balanced is better than being exalted.

Continuity is better than change.

Sparse is better than profuse.

Neutral is better than aggressive.

The obvious is better than that which must be sought.

Few elements are better than many.

A system is better than single elements.

Dieter Rams, 1987

Dieter Rams, the German industrial designer who worked for Braun electrical company, was a pioneer of the modernist movement. His work later became synonymous with 'quiet simplicity'.

focus away from the authority of 'high' culture. The 'mass media' seemed more relevant and more vital than 'fine art', particularly at the RCA in the 50s. Aestheticism, romanticism and high modernism paled beside the hybrid energies of urban life and the ad-men. Which is one distinctly potted version of the advent of Pop Art in England, with its appropriation of pop imagery and artefacts, and a kind of pre-emptive nostalgia for the signs and symbols of an ephemeral culture. (Much of it had taken on the feeling of dusty bygones in the Royal Academy's 1991 retrospective.)

We all know what it is, yet no two artists associated with Pop back then would later give the same account of it. Pop was not born with the term (first credited to Lawrence Alloway of the Independent Group in 1958), but shades backwards and forwards into collage and painterly abstraction on the one hand; on the other to Duchamp's 'ready-mades' and so, oddly, to Conceptualism and the gratuitous confusion of much contemporary imagery. All the same those were heady times, as the Beatles hit the scene, and call girls toppled governments.

How relevant to this artist, Pop with abstract connections in the 90s?[2] Not more so than a bird's nest or Felix the Cat.

But there is a sweet-and-wicked mixture of reverence and irreverence in Spiller that has some

One of the lonely

David Spillar ←   ↓

This is a catalogue for the artist David Spillar. Imagery is hidden in throwout pages under bold typographic sections. The grid is used to offset the text from the imagery, adding both rhythm and tension – themes championed by Joseph Müller-Brockman.

Design: Studio AS

He was born in 1942 in Dartford, north-west Kent – in the same year that the first British traditional jazz band, George Webb's Dixielanders, played their first gig from a coal cart along Bexley Heath Broadway. Coincidentally, that Thameside area, with its Rhythm Clubs and later trad jazz connections with the London art school scene, played a leading role in the birth of post-war English pop culture[1]. Peter Blake, a Pop Art pioneer at the Royal College of Art in the 50s, was also born in working-class Dartford ten years earlier. 'Pop culture was the life I actually led', Blake said. For David Spiller it must have been as close to home.

His mother was sixteen when she had her first child, David, the third, didn't meet his father until he was four, because of the war. Three more children followed, making a total of six. Home life?

I guess it was hard in a certain way, but my memory is my father holding me up to find a bird's nest. Not to destroy it, but to see how beautiful it was.

And David was always drawing – in the blank pages at the back of books bought in jumble sales with his mum.

Something I always loved doing in those books was making a path with a crayon through the words. I wonder whether I'm still doing that really, still looking around words, trying to find a path.

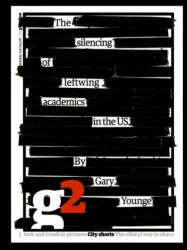

Right: The eyewitness double page spread is a regular feature of the Guardian newspaper. Breaking with tradition, the inclusion of a single image, with a small running caption, is startlingly poignant. This celebration of the power of an image creates a point of difference for the newspaper. A picture really does paint a thousand words.

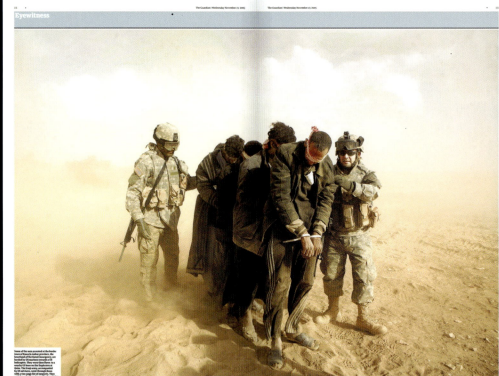

The Guardian   ← ↑

The change in technologies now means that newspapers need to deliver content in a printed and online form. Shared characteristics can be seen across these media through the relationship of colour (the blue banding) and typographic usage. The original broadsheet (typically 600mm high) was replaced with a more compact 'Berliner' format, which is notably shorter at around 470mm high. This popular European format effects changing social attitudes towards the convenience of a newspaper.

Design: Mark Porter

the perimeter

The perimeter is the area of margin space at the edge of a main layout. It can be used to frame a design by providing an area of clear space that offers a visual break and allows the design to breathe. On the other hand, the perimeter can be occupied. This occurs when design artwork bleeds off the page. The perimeter can use two or four margins of the page, a decision that can alter the dynamic of a design.

The passive
A passive perimeter adds a neutral element to a design, allowing the viewer's attention to focus on the active element within the layout – usually the content in the centre. The perimeter essentially frames the content with empty space to provide a calm setting, for example, a passepartout.

The active
An active perimeter typically involves just two of the margins and pulls the viewer's attention away from the centre of the page. It channels the visual element in the centre of the piece and allows it to run off the top and bottom of the page. In the example below, the content panel remains open and gives a sense of motion.

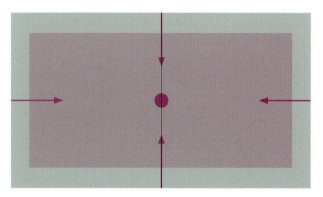

This layout has a passive perimeter that focuses attention on the central panel.

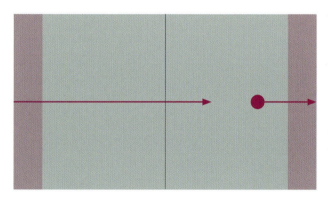

This layout has an active perimeter that leads the eye off the page, giving a sense of motion.

A design can feature a combination of active and passive elements that adds visual pace and pauses into a piece, which effectively alters how it is viewed.

Kefalonia Fisheries ← ↓

These designs feature active perimeters within which the artwork bleeds from the page to create excitement. The near life-size reproduction of the product demonstrates quality and freshness.

Design: Mouse Graphics

juxtaposition

Juxtaposition is the placement of different elements side by side in order to highlight or create contrasts. The word is derived from the Latin 'juxta', which means 'near'. Designers use juxtaposition to present ideas and to create or suggest relationships between them. These relationships may be based on elements having similar qualities such as shape, class, subject matter or some other shared ground.

Juxtaposition is a graphic device that may imply similarity or dissimilarity between items, which may only be clear from the context of the work as a whole. The juxtaposition of text and images can help to build a narrative in a design and communicate a message to the reader.

Juxtaposition draws a reader in and produces an active relationship with the design; viewers are not merely passive recipients of information. Juxtaposition challenges the viewer to identify the link between two or more elements that are placed side by side, and viewers are left to make the connections themselves.

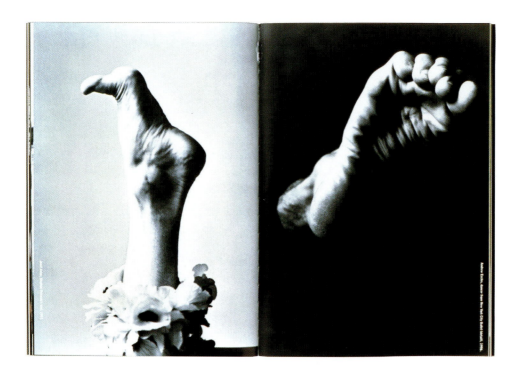

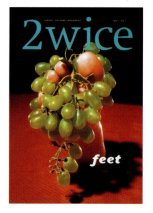

2wice ↑ ←

This spread features a juxtaposition of two similar things that are presented at different angles using various poses and lighting to create drama.

Design: Pentagram

The British Council ↑ →

These posters feature juxtaposed images of common themes in British culture, such as writing or football. These are juxtapositions based on time — one half of an image is from the past while the other half is contemporary.

Design: Johnson Banks

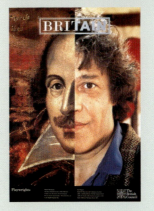

pace and hierarchy

Designers use layout to add pace to a design. This can be achieved by combining passive and active or busy and quiet pages. In this way, a designer is able to construct a narrative that the reader or viewer experiences as they advance through the publication or work. Full page photography and blank pages can provide a visual pause, in addition to illustrating the content.

Pace can be thought of as the momentum or motion that a design has over successive pages, whether in a document or website. Through considered layout planning, a design can create visual pauses for the reader – spaces to breathe in between pages that have more energy. Often, a visual pause may be used to signal a break between sections, chapters or different topics of information. Using thumbnails provides a designer with an overview of a design and allows them to judge and vary pace. The small images provide a view of the big picture and visual flow of a publication without being bogged down in the detail of each page.

Some types of content particularly lend themselves to and benefit from having changes in pace. Photography books often feature spreads with various pacing, changing from full-bleed images to pages containing several images. Conversely, a company brochure may be more concerned with allowing a reader to easily find something and so it would be counterproductive to change the layout design on every page.

A hierarchy can also be given to information through layout design. The prominence and amount of space given to text or images may make them seem more important than other elements presented at a smaller size. The location of an element in a publication and on a page is also suggestive of a hierarchy. Important items are usually positioned earlier and on a right-hand page towards the top left – the place where the eye naturally starts when viewing a new page.

A publication will normally have a hierarchy for text content that includes A heads, B heads, C heads and so on, each of which has different typographical styling that imparts an order of importance. This could be by a change of font, a change of weight, a change of typesize, a change of colour or a combination of these elements. A certain amount of restraint needs to be taken when creating a text hierarchy, otherwise the final result can become very chaotic. Implementing a text hierarchy does not mean abandoning a coherent typographical structure or order.

Thumbnails
An image or page of reduced size used as a visual reference. The use of thumbnails allows a designer to view several pages or images at once. Thumbnails can be used to get an idea of the sequence of a publication and its pace. Some designers will work in great detail on thumbnails, while others will simply use sticky notes so that they can move things around quickly.

64

COMBINING HIGH QUALITY
COFFEES FROM BRASIL WITH
THE DELICACY OF COFFEES
FROM COLUMBIA AND EL
SALVADOR, 64 PRODUCES
A SWEET, DELICATE TASTE
AND AROMA. WITH A ROUND,
FULL AND CREAMY FLAVOUR,
IT IS THE REFINED CHOICE
FOR ESPRESSO LOVERS.

ORIGIN	PROFILE	EXPERIENCE
South America and Central America.	Well-rounded and complex.	Balanced.

BIN 35

A VERY SWEET AND
COMPLEX DARK CARAMEL-
STYLE COFFEE, WITH A
MARMALADE FRUITINESS
AND THICK SYRUPY BODY.
AN AMAZING SINGLE ESTATE
COFFEE WITH INCREDIBLE
COMPLEXITY.

ORIGIN	PROFILE	EXPERIENCE
Australia.	Well-rounded and complex.	Balanced.

ORGANIC MEXICAN

COMPLEX, MELLOW
AND BALANCED, THESE
CERTIFIED ORGANIC BEANS
ARE SOFT ON THE PALATE
WITH MEDIUM ACIDITY AND
A MILD FINISH.

ORIGIN	PROFILE	EXPERIENCE
Central America.	Well-rounded and complex.	Balanced.

ORGANIC PERU

A WELL-ROUNDED, MEDIUM
TO FULL-BODIED VARIETY
WITH MILD ACIDITY.
THIS CERTIFIED ORGANIC
COFFEE IS SOURCED FROM
PLANTATIONS FARMED
BY DESCENDANTS OF
THE INCA CIVILISATION.

ORIGIN	PROFILE	EXPERIENCE
South America.	Well-rounded and complex.	Balanced.

BRASIL

A BOLD YET SMOOTH
TASTE WITH VELVETY BODY,
MILD, SWEET ACIDITY AND
A CHOCOLATE FINISH. OUR
BRASIL COFFEE IS SOURCED
EXCLUSIVELY FROM THE
DATERRA RESERVE—THE
CREAM OF EACH CROP.

ORIGIN	PROFILE	EXPERIENCE
South America.	Robust and vibrant.	Full-bodied.

Rio Coffee ← ↑

These examples feature a clear typographical hierarchy that is
established by the use of different typesizes and colour coding for
the various coffee products. While the layout of the publication is
the same from one page to the next, which makes digesting the text
information easy, pace is instilled into the design through the
emotions contained in the different images used.

Design: Voice

the Golden Section and Fibonacci Numbers

The Golden Section was thought by the ancients to represent infallibly beautiful proportions. Dividing a line by the approximate ratio of 8:13 means that the relationship of the longer part to the shorter is the same as that of the longer part to the whole. Objects that have this ratio are pleasing to the eye and can be found in a series of numbers called Fibonacci numbers. This ratio can be seen in nature in the growth patterns of plants and the shells of certain animals, such as snails. Perhaps it is because of its presence in nature that these proportions are so pleasing to the eye. In the field of graphic arts, the Golden Section is the basis for paper sizes and its principles can be used as a means of achieving balanced designs.

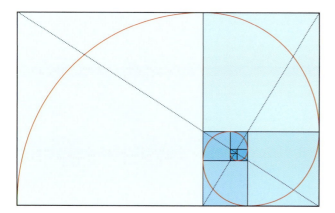

A set of Fibonacci rectangles and a Fibonacci spiral.

If you draw two small squares together, then draw another square using the combined lengths of the two squares as one side and carry on repeating this process you create a set of Fibonacci rectangles. This is a set of rectangles whose sides are two successive Fibonacci numbers in length, composed of squares with sides that are Fibonacci numbers, or in other words, the ratio of the sides of these rectangles equals that of the Golden Section.

A Fibonacci spiral can be created by drawing quarter circles through each square that together form the spiral. A similar curve occurs in nature in the shape of a snail's shell.

Pictured below is the sequence for drawing a Golden Section. Begin with a square (A) and bisect it (B). Then form a triangle (C) by drawing a line from the bottom of the bisecting line to the top corner of the square. With a compass, extend an arc from the apex of the triangle to the baseline (D) and draw a line perpendicular to the baseline from the point at which the arc intersects it. Complete the rectangle to form the Golden Section (E).

A

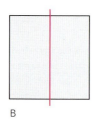

B

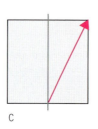

C

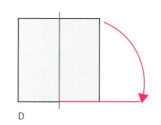

D

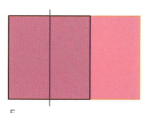

E

5	8	13	21	34	55	89	144
6	**10**	**16**	**26**	42	68	110	178
7	**11**	**18**	**29**	47	76	123	199

Fibonacci (aka Leonardo of Pisa), born in Pisa, Italy about 1175, has been called the greatest European mathematician of the Middle Ages because of a discovery he made that has excited natural biologists and mathematicians for hundreds of years. The series of numbers that bear his name, Fibonacci numbers, are also a cornerstone of design practice.

Fibonacci numbers are a series of numbers where each number is the sum of the preceding two. The series starting from zero can be seen below. Fibonacci numbers are important because of their link to the 8:13 ratio – also known as the Golden Section.

If you take two successive numbers in Fibonacci's series and divide the higher value by the one before it you get a number close to 1.6. For example 13/8 = 1.625. If you continued doing this through the series, the outcome hones in on a value that is approximately 1.61804 – the Golden Ratio, Golden Number or Golden Section.

0 1 1 2 3 5 8 13 21 34 55 89 144 233 377 610 987 1597 2584 4181 6765, 10,946 17,711

The Modulor

A harmonic measure to the human scale, universally applicable to architecture and mechanics, which has since been adopted by designers of all disciplines.

In 1947, Le Corbusier's Modulor system – protected by patent – was made public. The following year it appeared in his seminal book Le Modulor.

'A range of dimensions which makes the good easy and the bad hard.'

10 ten point type
11 on eleven point leading

16 sixteen point type
18 on eighteen point leading

26 twenty-six point type
29 on twenty-nine point leading

The modulor system is essentially a slide rule, with measurements derived from human proportions that can be used in design and construction. The relationship of human form to measurement creates a harmonious balance, be it in architecture, page sizes or even type. Often, more than one set of integers are used, as with the three examples of type and leading (above), which have been set to the values of two consecutive Fibonacci number systems.

baseline grid

The baseline grid is the graphic foundation on which a design is constructed. It serves a similar purpose to the scaffolding used in building construction, providing a means of support and a guide to positioning elements on the page with an accuracy that is difficult to achieve by eye alone.

Designing each page separately is time consuming and indulgent, but sometimes necessary. The grid helps proportion a page in both the vertical and horizontal planes, making the design process quicker and easier. Grids help to ensure visual consistency and explain how the design works. The grid will often vary throughout a publication to present different information in a variety ways.

The baseline grid has important relationships with many key elements of the design such as the baseline-to-baseline distance, and by implication, the typeface, size and leading. Another consideration is whether the grid is positioned to the x-height or cap height.

Grids are as much of a tool as a designer chooses them to be. Some feel the grid is their best friend while others find it restrictive. Flexibility

is important to make designs interesting and accessible — this is made possible by the complexity of the grid. We are familiar with a page

divided into columns, but adding a horizontal grid provides zones where text and images start. Complexity and freedom can be increased by

overlaying two or more grids that create odd spaces for elements to be positioned.

Simple grid structure showing:

1. Columns of type with lines depicted running top to bottom and bottom to top

2. Position of captions
3. Margin
4. Gutter

5. Position of running heads and chapter headers
6. Bleed

7. Position of folio
8. Baseline of text area
9. Trim size

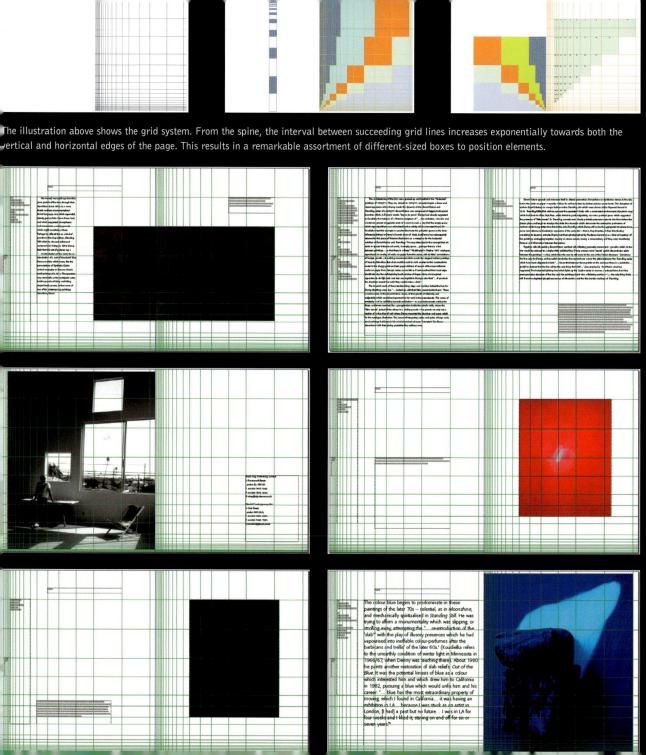

The illustration above shows the grid system. From the spine, the interval between succeeding grid lines increases exponentially towards both the vertical and horizontal edges of the page. This results in a remarkable assortment of different-sized boxes to position elements.

The colour blue begins to predominate in these paintings of the later 70s — celestial, as in *Moonshine*, and mechanically spiritualised in *Standing Still*. He was trying to affirm a monumentality which was slipping, or strolling away, attempting the "... re-introduction of the 'slab'" with the play of illusory presences which he had vaporised into ineffable colour-perfumes after the barbicans and trellis' of the later 60s.' (Koudielka refers to the unearthly condition of winter light in Minnesota in 1966/67, when Denny was teaching there). About 1980 he paints another restoration of slab reliefs *Out of the Blue*. It was the potential kinesis of blue as a colour which interested him and which drew him to California in 1982, pursuing a blue which would unfix him and his career: "... blue has the most extraordinary property of moving which I found in California... it was having an exhibition in LA... because I was stuck as an artist in London, [I had] a past but no future... I was in LA for four weeks and I liked it, staying on and off for six or seven years."

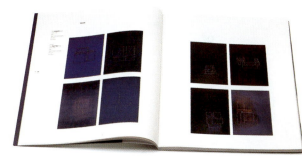

Robyn Denny ← ↑

The illustrations (top left) show the complex grid system used to produce the publication. From the spine, the interval between succeeding grid lines increases exponentially towards both the vertical and horizontal edges of the page, which results in a remarkable assortment of different-sized boxes to position elements. As no two boxes have the same dimensions, there is unlimited scope for creative positioning of text boxes, images, titles, footers, captions and folios while maintaining order and structure. The resulting book is deceptively simple as content in varying configurations is accommodated with ease due to the grid.

Design: Studio AS

Active and passive / Looking closer

Exercise #1 – Active and passive

Premise
An image can be presented in an active or passive way. A designer can change this through the way a spread is composed and how the elements are arranged.

Exercise
Select two images or photographs and try different compositions to make them active and passive elements in the design.

Outcome
Produce a visualization of your findings highlighting the active and passive results you have identified.

Aim
To encourage a more considered appreciation of how the active and passive use of images affects how a design communicates.

Active and passive ↓

The illustration below shows how different compositions can make the use of photos passively or actively. Positioning, cropping and juxtaposition can all change the final outcome.

Exercise #2 – Looking closer

Premise
We are familiar with grid-based layouts in books and magazines, but layouts are all around us. They are present everywhere that there is visual and textural communication, such as signage.

Exercise
Undertake an audit on the layouts that you find in the environment and identify the patterns and structures you see. Are all recipe books similar? Do signs structure information in the same way? Why does it make sense for some items to use centred layouts as opposed to range left?

Outcome
Produce a visualization that shows the layouts you identified and a sketch or thumbnail of the basic grid they employ to structure their information. State why they are effective for the content concerned.

Aim
To encourage a more considered appreciation of the power of layouts and how they are used to present different pieces of information.

Layout in use   ↑

The above two images display different types of information that we may encounter on any given day. They have different layouts but are both structured around a grid.

LET'S ROCK
sweet gene vincent

WARDROBE

ROCK STYLE

> 05 october 2000 to 14 january 2001
> Barbican Gallery

Sponsored by new green from American Express

FAN-TASTIC
FANS, GRAPHICS, JUKE BOX
T-SHIRTS, DOCUMENTARIES

HEY DJ

PERFORMANCE
HOMAGE TO BOWIE, MADONNA AND BJÖRK
AND THEIR CHAMELEON ARTISTRY

TOP 30 ICONS

TRANSFORM

DARE YOU TRY IT ON?

DISPLAY
hip, cool + classic pieces of clothing

LEATHER

INDIE/RAVES

PUNK

SEX

HIP HOP

FUNK

MOD

Let's face it, style has always been inextricable from pop. Without style, rock music wouldn't exist; without fashion, pop doesn't work. Without the razzle dazzle of satin and tat, pop music is just a badly tuned radio. Rock Style is a cultural symbiosis, a mutually beneficial means to an end. Without his ducktail and his finger tip drapes Elvis Presley was just another greasy trucker with ambitions beyond his station; without their collarless suits and mop-top fringes the Beatles were simply another beat band (albeit one which originated its own material); and without a pantechnicon full of costume changes, Madonna was just another jumped-up waitress with more mouth than was good for her. Without their costumes Kiss were just another heads-down-see-you-at-the-end heavy rock act; without Stone Island and CP Company Oasis were just the sound of a rebellion in the dark; and without his white silk socks, Michael Jackson was just another freewheeling minstrel. Not only have rock and pop stars always taken street fashion to its logical extremes — encapsulating time and time again the allure of street credibility — but they've also influenced every new generation since WWII. Sometimes these Tin Pan Alley Valentinos come fully formed — think Elvis, Ziggy Stardust, Sid Vicious or Marilyn Manson — and sometimes they just pick up the baton and run with it. Either way Rock Style has become the defining culture of the early 21st century. Only 50 years of age, it has grown, metamorphosed and reinvented itself so many times that being an individual these days is sometimes just about enough to make it as a pop star. Whether you'll make it as a pop hero is open to debate, but as Andy Warhol once said, in the future, everyone will be famous for 15 minutes. Well, the future's right now.

Barbican Centre

Typography

Typography is the means by which a written idea is given visual form. The selection of the visual form can dramatically affect the readability of the written idea and a reader's feelings towards it. There are hundreds, if not thousands, of typefaces available. Typography can produce a neutral effect or rouse passions, symbolize artistic, political or philosophical movements, or express the personality of a person or organization. Typefaces vary from clear and distinguishable letterforms that flow easily before the eye and are suitable for extended blocks of text, to more dramatic and eye-catching typefaces that grab attention, such as in newspaper headlines and advertisements.

Many typefaces in use today are based upon designs created during earlier historic epochs. Typography continues to evolve and accelerate as technology makes typeface design quicker and easier, whether creating something novel or adapting something from an earlier era.

Rock Style ←

The exhibition design and graphics for the Rock Style exhibition at the Barbican Centre, London features a fanzine design style that mimics the exhibition's content. It uses hand-drawn typography and collected ephemera that form an overall graphic style.

Design: Studio Myerscough

type

Type size is the vertical size of the body of a typographical character including the space above and below its strokes. Type size is commonly thought of as the size of the typeface, but it historically refers to the size of the body or block that holds the printing face of a metal typographical character in the days of letterpress printing. A character is always slightly smaller than its given type size because of this. Type sizes for body text are usually 8pt to 14pt; different type sizes are used within a design to indicate a hierarchy of importance as we tend to read larger type sizes first.

6 7 8 9 10 11 12 14 16 18 21 24 36 48 60 72

Point system

The point system is used to specify the typographical dimensions of a page. This is represented in points and picas. The British and American system is based on an imperial point with dimensions as follows: the point is 1/72 of an inch. There are 12 points to a pica, about six picas to an inch. The pica is used for linear measurement of type including line lengths.

12 points = 1 pica
1 point = 0.35mm
1 pica = 4.22mm

The European Didot system is slightly different but provides similar values:

12 Didot = 1 Cicero
1 Didot = 0.38mm
1 Cicero = 4.56mm

There are 12 points to a pica, about six picas to an inch. The pica is used for linear measurement of type. The length of a line is specified in picas.

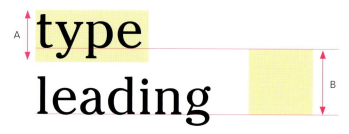

Typography uses points to describe type size (A) and the leading value (B). Type size is the size of the bounding box rather than the height of a letter. Leading is a hot metal printing term that originates from the lead strips that were inserted between text measures in order to space them evenly. Nowadays, the leading value represents the distance from one base line to the next, rather than the actual space between the lines of text. Typographic measurements normally have two values. For example, 10pt Helvetica with 4pt leading is expressed as 10/14 Helvetica – 10 'on' 14. Type with no extra leading is said to be 'set solid'.

The em, the en and relative measurements

Various measurements in typography, such as character spacing, are relative measurements that are linked to the type size of the font being used rather than being absolute measurements in points or millimetres. The use of relative measurements helps ensure that a piece of text looks harmonious and in proportion.

Ems and ens are relative measurements that have no prescribed, absolute size. Their size is relative to the size of type that is being set. An em is a basic unit of measurement for a given typeface derived from the width of its upper-case letter 'M'. The term originates from when type was cast in metal and the letter 'M' was cast on a square body. As the letter 'M' was originally as wide as the type size, an em has the same point size as the typeface. The em is used as a constant against which to base other typographical measurements, such as the set width, which is how much horizontal space a given amount of copy will occupy in a given type size. The em is also used for paragraph indents, fixed spacing and an em dash – a dash one em in length. An en is half of an em and so an en dash is half the length of an em dash. Nowadays, with computer-generated typefaces, the letter 'M' now has no relation to the em measurement.

Most desktop publishing programs automatically assign relative leading values. For example, the leading value may be set at 120% and so it will change relative to increases or decreases in the type size. If this did not happen and leading remained constant, as the type size increases the characters would eventually crash into one another.

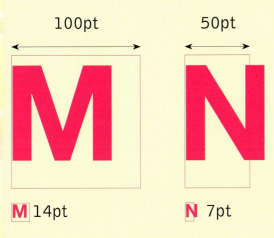

100pt   50pt

M 14pt   N 7pt

Em and en

An em is a unit of measure equal to the width and height of the point size of the type being set. So type of 100pts uses an em of 100pts, and 14pt type uses an em of 14pts.

An en is a measurement that follows the same origins as the em and is equal to half the point size of a typeface. So type of 100pts uses an en of 50pts, and type of 14pts uses an en of seven pts.

legibility of typefaces

Legibility of typefaces

Legibility is a type characteristic that allows us to distinguish one letterform from another through the physical traits inherent in a particular typeface, such as its x-height, character shapes, counter size, stroke contrast and type weight. For example, newspaper fonts have high stroke weight contrast and condensed forms to ensure legibility and the efficient use of space. This term is often confused with readability, which concerns the properties of a piece of type or design that affect the ability to understand it.

The subheading above is set in Cheltenham 1896. It was designed with exaggerated ascenders and descenders as studies into the legibility of typefaces had shown that readers scanned text using the tops of letters. Although the bottom part of the letters in this subheading have been removed, it can still be read relatively easily.

anatomy of a typeface

Typefaces and type families can be classified according to their inherent characteristics. Many typefaces originate in designs from the past 500 years that would have originally been cast in metal. Other typefaces have a lineage that goes back to the work of stonemasons. Although now in digital format, such typefaces still contain distinct elements associated with the physical necessities of the times in which they were created. The digital age has led to an explosion of the number of typefaces available and has made it simpler to design a new typeface or alter an existing one.

Roman

The basic letterform. So called as the origins of the letter are in the inscriptions found on Roman monuments. Some typefaces also carry a slightly lighter version called 'Book' (see below).

Italic and oblique

An italic is a drawn version of the Roman cut that has an angled axis, for example 'a'. Most typefaces have an italic family member. An oblique is a slanted version of a sans-serif typeface and is not newly drawn.

Light

A lighter version of the Roman cut.

Condensed

Condensed is a narrower version of the Roman cut.

Boldface

Uses a wider stroke than the Roman. It is also known as Medium, Semibold, Black, Super (as in the case of Akzidenz Grotesk) and Poster, as found with Bodoni.

Extended

Extended type is a wider version of the Roman cut.

There is no standard or convention for naming the different weights or cuts of a typeface and so they may have different names. For example, 'heavy', 'black' and 'extra' all describe typefaces with heavier weights and thicker strokes than the basic Roman typeface. The basic or normal weight may also be called 'regular' or 'book', as well as Roman.

Demi

A weight that is between the roman and boldface weights. Sometimes called Demi Bold, it uses wider strokes than Roman, but is thinner than Boldface.

Book

An upright typeface that is suitable for lengthy texts, such as books. Often used as a synonym for Roman.

Apex   Bowl   Arm

Bar   Stress   Stroke

Hairline

Tail

Ascender   Counter   Stem

Ear

Shoulder   Link   Loop

Height of ascenders

Depth of descenders

Serif

Terminal

x-Height

describing type

Typography has a rich lexicon that describes its various aspects. Below are some of these typographic terms.

MAJUSCULE

Refers to uppercase or capital letters. Above is a typeface called Trajan and it is only available as upper case (known as omnicase or unicase).

minuscule

Refers to lower case or sentence letters.

Swash Characters

These have extended or exaggerated decorative calligraphic swashes, usually on capitals.

SMALL CAPS

Majuscules that are closer in size to the minuscule characters of a given typeface, which are less domineering than regular capitals. Small caps are used for setting acronyms and common abbreviations. Also called Petite Caps in certain fonts such as Mrs Eaves (above).

Ligatures

The joining of separate characters to form a single unit to avoid interference in certain combinations (see page 81).

Display or Poster

Large and/or distinctive type intended to attract the eye. Specifically cut to be viewed from a distance. Shown above is Bodoni Poster.

CamelCase

Where the initial letter of a compound word is capitalized. Also called MedialCapitals or InterCaps, this technique is used extensively in logos.

PI characters

These are Greek letters used as mathematical symbols, for example: Σ, $\sqrt{}$, f, 1/2, 1/4, 1/8, $, ¥, £.

Dingbats

A collection of special decorative characters and symbols. Dingbats can include symbols ✖, icons ☝ or decorative items ❀.

unicase

A typeface that only has one case rather than sets of majuscule and minuscule characters. Unicase characters tend to be more similar to minuscules. The type shown is Bayer Universal.

Script

A typeface designed to imitate handwriting. It typically consists of flourishes such as swashes and finials on majuscules, which joins the letters. Shown above is Künstler Script.

INLINE

Also called 'hand tooled', these fonts often have decorative designs on the front face. The above type is Rosewood.

this is *my* **habitat**

Habitat ↑ ←

Knowing what typeface to use is one of the cruxes of typographic design. Here, a simple mixture of weights and colours creates a friendly, inviting atmosphere.

Design: Propaganda

classification systems

Typeface classification is one of the few occasions when it is appropriate to make judgements based on appearance. It is important to obtain an appreciation of how typefaces are classified, and the differences between them, in order to understand when to best use them. As there are many systems for classification this section will address the most commonly known classification classes, which often have several different names.

Loosely speaking, fonts are classified based on their characteristics. There are four basic categories of typefaces: Roman, Gothic, Script and Block (Sanders and McCormick: Human Factors in Engineering and Design, 1993). In general terms, Roman is the class where we find all serif fonts; Gothic fonts are sans serif; the Script category is for typefaces that mimic handwriting; and Blackletter is for fonts based on German manuscript handwriting.

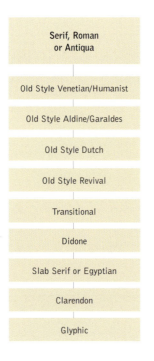

Blackletter, Gothic, Old English, Block or Broken

Serif, Roman or Antiqua

Old Style Venetian/Humanist

Old Style Aldine/Garaldes

Old Style Dutch

Old Style Revival

Transitional

Didone

Slab Serif or Egyptian

Clarendon

Glyphic

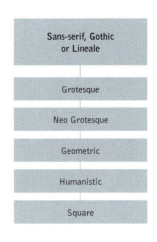

Sans-serif, Gothic or Lineale

Grotesque

Neo Grotesque

Geometric

Humanistic

Square

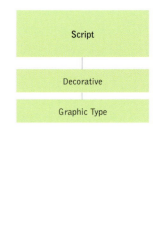

Script

Decorative

Graphic Type

The above classification is very much a first cut and tells little other than the most basic information about a typeface. Each class can be further divided into subclasses that provide more specific information.

Blackletter is based on the heavy, ornate writing style prevalent during the Middle Ages. Due to the complexity of the letters they may be hard to read, particularly in large blocks of text. They are commonly used for similar purposes as the scripts — as initial caps and on certificates. Recent research, however, has found that legibility is linked to familiarity, and the sans serif style of today would be equally illegible to Middle Age man.

Literally translated as 'broken writing', Fraktur was the prominent calligraphic style for centuries. Although no longer used for body copy, this distinctive typeface conveys a feeling of historical importance.

Research has shown that the barely noticeable serifs greatly aid our recognition of the characters and help us to read by leading the eye across the line of text. For this reason, body text is easier to read in a serif font.

Goudy Modern 1918 F W Goudy Clear directional serifs create a legible font.

Sans serifs, as the name suggests, do not have decorative touches that lead the eye so long passages in these typefaces can be difficult to read. However, sans serifs have been designed for use as body text. Their clean and simple design makes them ideal for display text such as headlines, captions and other non-body text uses.

Helvetica 1959 Max Miedinger Typeface was formerly called Neue Haas Grotesk.

Script typefaces were designed to imitate handwriting so that when printed the characters appear to be joined up. The writing implements they replicate range from a fountain pen to a paintbrush and, as with handwriting, text should not be all in capitals. These fonts are commonly seen in short bursts such as on invitations, business cards and in advertisements.

Brody 1953 Harold Broderson — very short descenders, with close-fitting lower-case letters.

ANOTHER GENERAL TYPEFACE CATEGORY NEEDS TO BE MENTIONED – SYMBOL – AS SOME FONTS DO NOT FIT INTO THE BASIC CLASSIFICATION SYSTEM SHOWN ON THE PREVIOUS PAGE. THIS INCLUDES DECORATIVE, DISPLAY, EXPERIMENTAL OR GRAPHIC TYPEFACES THAT CANNOT READILY BE ASSIGNED TO THE OTHER CLASSIFICATIONS, SUCH AS THOSE SHOWN OPPOSITE.

Stencil 1937 Gerry Powell
Utilitarian packaging-inspired typeface that comes only in upper case.

Symbol

Zapf Dingbats 1978 Hermann Zapf

Designed to complement contemporary typefaces, several traditional symbols are given a modern interpretation, including the dagger and the pilcrow.

Experimental

Flixel Just van Rossum

A font questioning the link between legibility and communication.

Decorative

ABCDEFGHIJKLMNOPQRSTUVWXYZ

Rosewood 1994 Kim Buker Chansler, Carl Crossgrove and Carol Twombly

An ornate circus-inspired in-line decorative typeface.

Graphic

ABCDEFGHIJKLMNOPQRSTUVWXYZ

American Typewriter 1974 Joel Kaden and Tony Stan

Font designed to replicate the appearance of hand-typed text.

Optical character recognition

ABCDEFGHIJKLMNOPQRSTUVWXYZ

OCR–A 1968 ATF

Designed to meet the requirements of the European Computer Manufacturers Association (ECMA).

extended type families

An extended type family is all the variations of a particular typeface or font. It includes all the different weights, widths and italics. Examples of family names are Univers, Times Roman, Arial and Garamond. Many type families are named after their creator or the publication in which they were first used.

Type families are a useful design tool because they offer a designer a range of variations that work together in a clean and consistent way. To achieve clarity and a uniform feel to a piece of work, many designers restrict themselves to using only two type families for a project, meeting their requirements from the type variations these contain to establish the typographic hierarchy. For example, from the six variations of the Officina family on the opposite page, you can pick out typefaces for use as titles, body text and captions.

ABCDEFGHIJKLMNOPQRSTUVWXYZ
abcdefghijklmnopqrstuvwxyz 1234567890

ABCDEFGHIJKLMNOPQRSTUVWXYZ
abcdefghijklmnopqrstuvwxyz 1234567890

Rotis 1988 Otl Aicher
A font that offers many weights with interchangeable serifs.

The Sans The Mix

The Sans/The Mix 1994–1999 Lucas de Groot
Fonts that offer a great range of weights and serif options.

ABCDEFGHIJKLMNOPQRSTUVWXYZ
abcdefghijklmnopqrstuvwxyz 1234567890

ABCDEFGHIJKLMNOPQRSTUVWXYZ
abcdefghijklmnopqrstuvwxyz 1234567890

ABCDEFGHIJKLMNOPQRSTUVWXYZ
abcdefghijklmnopqrstuvwxyz 1234567890

ABCDEFGHIJKLMNOPQRSTUVWXYZ
abcdefghijklmnopqrstuvwxyz 1234567890

ABCDEFGHIJKLMNOPQRSTUVWXYZ
abcdefghijklmnopqrstuvwxyz 1234567890

ABCDEFGHIJKLMNOPQRSTUVWXYZ
abcdefghijklmnopqrstuvwxyz 1234567890

Officina (top to bottom: Sans Book, Sans Book Italic, Sans Bold, Serif Book, Serif Book Italic, Serif Bold) 1990 Erik Spiekermann
Originally designed for use on office documentation and stationery.

typographic colour

Typographic colour refers to the extent that type fills or colours a given space based on the density of its different typefaces and weights. **In simple terms, the heavier the weight the denser the type will appear, hence giving more colour. Using bold, or even black, will give a type increased presence on the page. Combined with letter and word spacing, this will help to influence typographic colour.**

Olympic Air →

This magazine aimed at air travellers shows how typographic colour affects the design. The magazine is a dual language publication and the colour and weight of each language creates a different density or texture.

Design: Mouse Graphics

The Archive ↙ ↓

This website for furniture and accessories shows how 'colour' exists, even in a monotone design. Here, the confident use of typography adds texture through the use of type weights.

Design: Beetroot

IO
mysti
cal
travel
destina
tions

Από την Κάλλια Καστάνη_By Kallia Kastani

(μέρος a | part a)

Μνημεία Παγκόσμιας Πολιτιστικής και Φυσικής Κληρονομιάς, τόποι άγριας ομορφιάς που συνδέονται με θρύλους, αινίγματα, μυστηριακές λατρείες, ή μέρη παραμυθένια, που η ύπαρξή τους και μόνο μοιάζει να καταργεί τη λογική σειρά του κόσμου. Hereux qui comme Ulysse, a fait un beau voyage...

World Monuments of Cultural and Natural Heritage and wild beauty, linked to legends, mysteries, mystical ceremonies, or enchanted destinations whose mere existence seems to contradict the natural order of the universe. Hereux qui comme Ulysse, a fait un beau voyage...

Μνημείο Παγκόσμιας Κληρονομιάς (Πολιτιστικής ή Φυσικής) της UNESCO είναι κάθε τόπος (π.χ., δάσος, βουνό, λίμνη, έρημος, μνημείο, κτίριο, σύμπλεγμα κ.λπ.) που χαρακτηρίζεται από τον Οργανισμό ως «ιδιαίτερης πολιτιστικής ή φυσικής σημασίας». Δηλαδή, μια αναντικατάστατη κληρονομιά για την ανθρωπότητα, που είναι προς το συμφέρον της να διατηρηθεί – είτε γιατί είναι εξαιρετικής ομορφιάς είτε γιατί αποτελεί αριστούργημα της ανθρώπινης δημιουργικής ευφυΐας είτε επειδή συνιστά μαρτυρία μιας παράδοσης ή ενός πολιτισμού που έχει χαθεί... Από το 2009, στη σχετική λίστα της UNESCO περιλαμβάνονται 890 μνημεία σε 148 κράτη. Απ' αυτά, τα 17 είναι ελληνικά, σε σύνολο 400 περίπου ευρωπαϊκών. Σε κάθε γωνιά της Γηραιάς Ηπείρου παραμονεύει και ένα μικρό θαύμα... Διαλέξαμε τα 10 κορυφαία και σας τα παρουσιάζουμε ανά 5, σ' αυτό και στο επόμενο τεύχος.

A UNESCO World Heritage Site (Cultural or Natural) is a place (such as a forest, mountain, lake, desert, monument, building, complex, or city) that is listed by UNESCO as being of "special cultural or physical significance." In other words, it represents an irreplaceable part of the common heritage of humanity, and it is in its best interests that this site be preserved – either because of its exceptional natural beauty and aesthetic importance, because it is a masterpiece of human creative genius, because its bears exceptional testimony to a cultural tradition which has disappeared... As of 2009, UNESCO lists 890 sites in 148 states. Out of a total of about 400 World Heritage Sites in Europe, 17 of these are located in Greece. There is a little miracle located in almost every corner of the Old Continent.

type generation

While there are thousands of typefaces available, it is sometimes necessary to generate new ones. Font creation can be as complex as creating original art, or as simple as replicating and adapting found type from older publications. The two main approaches to generating new typefaces are to draw them and to render them in a font generation program. The ability to create fonts electronically has made it possible to generate fonts quickly in response to the specific needs and desires of clients, designers and typographers.

To draw

Type can be drawn or crafted by hand to produce something personal, idiosyncratic, unique and analogue. Hand-drawn type can be viewed as mark-making to create characters very attuned to a specific use.

To render

The geometric capabilities of computer software and their use of vectors mean fonts can be generated and tweaked rapidly to create a new set of characters.

Kalathaki Lemnos ↑

This packaging features hand-drawn Greek characters that communicate and emphasize the personal, family nature of the producer conveying the messages that this product is crafted rather than mass produced.

Design: Beetroot

Venue ↑

This identity for a betting shop chain features rendered characters. The designer was able to experiment and try out several versions of the 'e' before selecting the final one, which has a unique treatment of the counter. The glyph 'u' plays a pivotal role – it also means 'you' and puts the customer at the centre of the proposition. The 'u' is also similar in form to a horseshoe – a symbol of luck appropriate to the service offered.

Design: Gavin Ambrose / Adrian Sharman

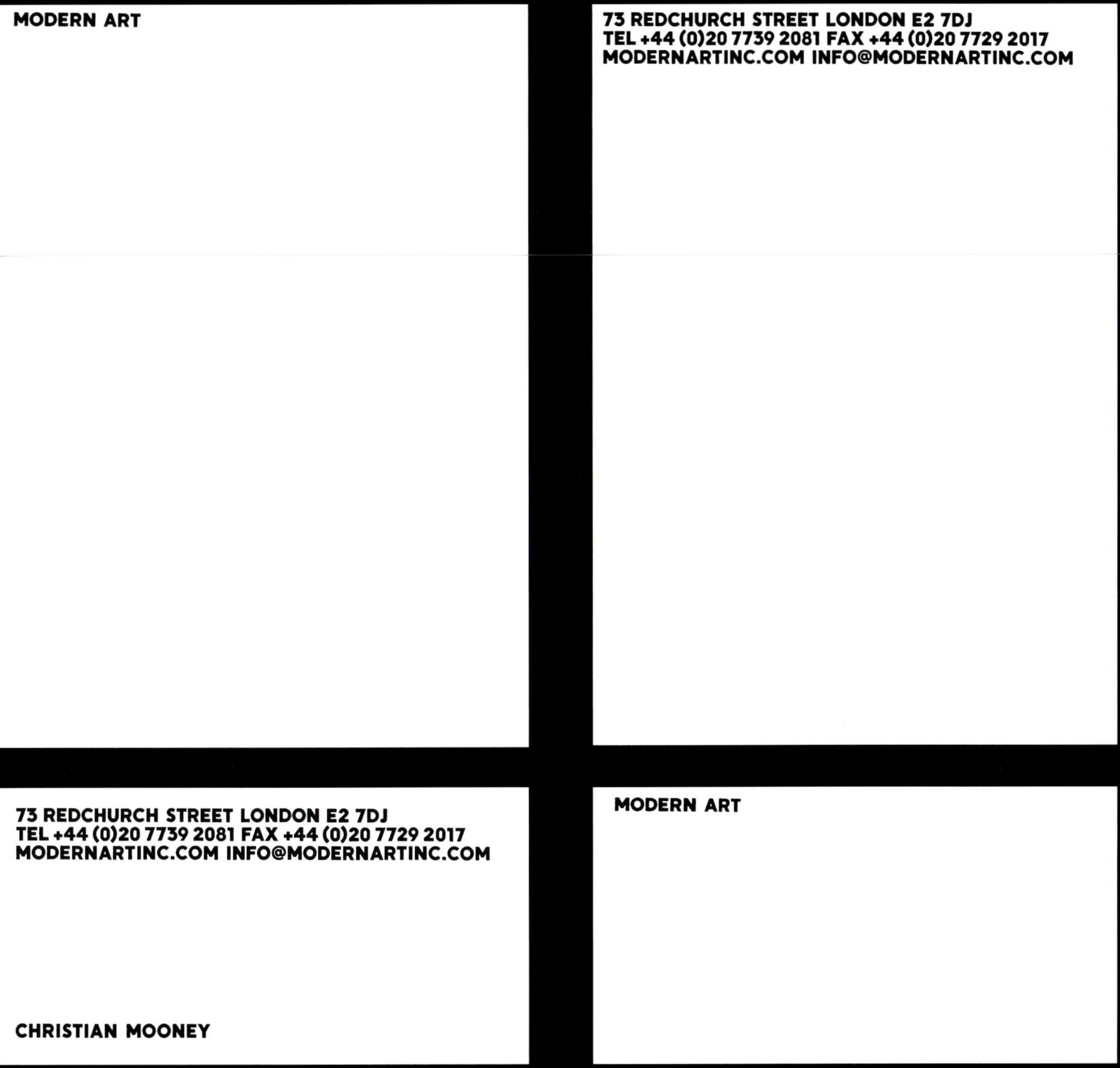

MODERN ART

73 REDCHURCH STREET LONDON E2 7DJ
TEL +44 (0)20 7739 2081 FAX +44 (0)20 7729 2017
MODERNARTINC.COM INFO@MODERNARTINC.COM

73 REDCHURCH STREET LONDON E2 7DJ
TEL +44 (0)20 7739 2081 FAX +44 (0)20 7729 2017
MODERNARTINC.COM INFO@MODERNARTINC.COM

MODERN ART

CHRISTIAN MOONEY

Modern Art   ↑

This identity for Modern Art, a contemporary art gallery in London's East End, features a bespoke typeface (Standard Modern) that has majuscule characters. The various pieces – including business cards, letterheads, continuation sheets, complimentary slips, signage and regular preview cards – were printed using a letterpress.

Design: Blue Source

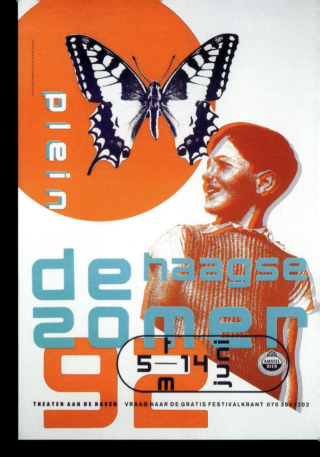

De Haagse Zomer ← ↖

These posters for the De Haagse Zomer (The Hague Summer Festival feature strong visual images that enable them to stand out among other posters displayed in a city. Bright colours and images from old magazines were cut and pasted together by hand. The typography was taken from old typeface manuals and inspired by pioneers such as Piet Zwart en Schuitema in Holland and Russian constructivists such El Lissitzky and Rodchenko. However, the studio added its own twist, making explicit use of the edge of the poster, and using typography of immediate and striking effect.

Design: Faydherbe / de Vringer

ABCDEFGHIJKLMNOPQRSTUVWXYZ
abcdefghijklmnopqrstuvwxyz
0123456789!?,"£$&%@*

Yellow regular

ABCDEFGHIJKLMNOPQRSTUVWXYZ
abcdefghijklmnopqrstuvwxyz
0123456789!?,"£$&%@*

Yellow bold

Yellow pages ↓ ←

When Yellow Pages redesigned their listings of names, addresses and contact details, typography was a cornerstone. The old typeface was difficult to read, especially at small point sizes and so this redesign concentrated on type generation that focused on details and the printing limitations of huge volume printing. The characters were carefully created to be more legible at small sizes and to allow more information to go onto a line. Special features included a condensed basic form of type with ascenders and descenders at 75% of normal height and junctions chiselled away to allow for ink fill at very small type sizes.

Design: Johnson Banks

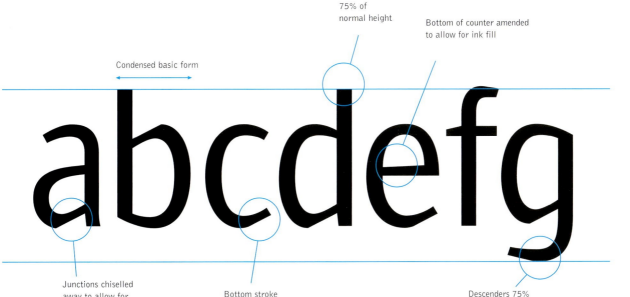

Ascenders 75% of normal height

Bottom of counter amended to allow for ink fill

Condensed basic form

Junctions chiselled away to allow for fill in at very small type sizes

Bottom stroke thinned to allow for ink spread

Descenders 75% of normal height

vertical and horizontal spacing

Text can be positioned in different ways within a text box to give different vertical and horizontal treatments and presentations.

Top aligned
This text is aligned to the top of the text block, the typical default text position.

Bottom aligned
This text is aligned to the bottom of the text block.

Centred vertically
This text is aligned to the centre of the text block; often used for headings, captions and pull quotes.

Justified vertically
This text has been vertically justified to force the lines to distribute throughout the vertical extent of the text block.

Text can be set to align with either the top, bottom or centre of a text block, and in extreme examples it will be justified, that is to say it will align with both the top and the bottom of the text block (shown above). Secondly, additional spacing can be added between lines, called leading, that will produce different 'setting' as shown below:

If type is set solid (without additional spaces) there is a certain amount of white space above and below the text because some is incorporated as part of each typeface to accommodate ascenders and descenders, and to prevent different lines being too jammed together. Leading is used to add extra space on the bottom of each line of type, typically to make it easier to read.

10pt type on 11pt leading

This paragraph is set with the default leading value of 120%, which for 10pt type is 12pt leading. Using the 120% default is fine for 10pt type as it produces a whole number for the leading. For 23pt type, however, the leading value of 27.6pt becomes irregular. In such cases, it is often easier to input a more convenient leading value such as 28pt.

10pt type on 12pt leading

Whilst there is a general default for leading of about 120% (that is, the leading value is 120% of the type point size), one can theoretically use any leading value at all. For a more extreme presentation, negative leading values can be used when using digital type so that text lines overlap.

10pt type on 7pt leading

If too much leading is used to set a text block, the individual text lines can become too separated making it harder to read because the eye does not track efficiently from one line to the next. The white space can also dominate and overwhelm the visual presence or colour of the text.

10pt type on 18pt leading

Measure

When setting type, we often refer to the measure. The measure of a text column is its width or line length. The absolute length of a measure will differ according to the typeface used and the typesize it is set in, as a measure is a relative measurement that refers to a certain amount of characters rather than an absolute distance. Type set using a font with a narrow set width will look different to text set with a wide set width. Changing the typeface will alter the width setting and may call for adjustment of the measure. While one type may give a relatively comfortable fit in the measure, another may have awkward spacing issues. Changing the size of the measure will make a column wider or narrower and so it will fill vertical space in a different way.

The three elements of measure, typesize and typeface are linked in that a change to any of them means that an adjustment may be needed in the others. As types of a given size do not share the same width, switching from one typeface to another will alter the setting of the type.

Characters per line

As a general rule, type on a wider measure will appear heavier and will benefit from additional leading. Notice how the column below right looks darker than the column below left, yet they are the same type size and leading value.

12 pica column

If type is set solid (without additional spaces) there is white space above and below the text because some is incorporated as part of each typeface to accommodate ascenders and descenders, and to prevent different lines being too jammed together.

24 pica column

Leading is used to add extra space on the bottom of each line of type, typically to make it easier to read. Leading is named after the strips of lead that performed this function on a letterpress; it is expressed in points. Type size and leading may be annotated as 10/12 Garamond, meaning the Garamond type size is 10 point, the distance between the baselines is 12 point, so the leading is therefore 2 point. 10/10 Garamond signifies no leading. Differences in typefaces mean the effect of leading will depend on its point size and x-height.

There are several ways to determine a text measure that will produce a comfortable line length to read, which is neither too long nor too short.

Option 1

The optimum line length is around nine words, based on the average word being five characters in length.

Lorem ipsum dolor sit amet, autem zzril elit, sed

Option 2

The optimum line length is around one and a half times the length of the lower case alphabet.

abcdefghijklmnopqrstuvwxyzabcdefghijklm

Option 3

Around 26 characters is considered minimum, 38 optimum, and 68 maximum.

abcdefghijklmnopqrstuvwxyz

abcdefghijklmnopqrstuvwxyzabcdefghijklm

abcdefghijklmnopqrstuvwxyzabcdefghijklmnopqrstuvwxyzabcdefghijklmnop

We also need to choose how we are aligning text in the horizontal plane.

<table>
<tr><td>

Aligned left
This alignment follows the principle of handwriting, with text tight and aligned to the left margin and ending ragged on the right.

</td><td>

Aligned right
Right aligning text is less common as it is more difficult to read. It is sometimes used for picture captions and other accompanying texts as it is clearly distinct from body copy.

</td><td>

Centred
Centred aligns each line horizontally to form a symmetrical shape on the page, with line beginnings and endings ragged. Raggedness can be controlled by adjusting line endings.

</td><td>

Justified
Justified text inserts space so that it extends to both the left and right margins. This may allow the appearance of rivers of unsightly white space to appear.

</td></tr>
</table>

And finally, we also need to consider how we space individual words, letters and particular characters:

Tracking or letterspacing

Tracking or letterspacing adjusts the space between characters, allowing a designer to open up crowded text. However, the addition of too much space between letters can make text look disjointed as words increasingly dissemble. An interesting setting quirk is that as type gets larger, for example for a poster, more space needs to be taken out not put in. **Tracking values do not necessarily hold true between typefaces as different fonts have different characteristics and stroke weights that affect their typographic colour and spacing.**

This type is set loose
This type is set normal
This type is set tight
This type is set overlapping

Word spacing

The distance between words – word spacing – can be increased or decreased while leaving the spacing between the letters of the words unaltered. Word spacing is used in particular when setting justified text to produce a balanced look to text blocks. Increasing word spacing will result in a 'whiter' body of text; conversely, decreasing it will result in a more solid or 'grey' appearance. Generally speaking, the wider the measure of text, the more space can be added. A book, for example, will often have more space between words than a magazine or newspaper, which tend to be more compact.

Normal word spacing

Reduced word spacing

Increased word spacing

Kerning

Kerning is the removal of space between characters. Kern originally referred to part of a character that extended outside its bounding block or printing block. Kerning is used to reduce unsightly space between two letters to give a more pleasing visual appearance. In the example (see right), the space between the 'k' and the 'e' has been reduced. Notice how this joins the 'k' to the word.

Without kerning – the k appears disjointed

kerning

With kerning – the k is connected to the rest of the word

kerning

Text justification and hyphenation

Special attention needs to be paid when justifying type, particularly when a narrow measure is used. Consecutive hyphenation, widows, irregular spacing (white acne) and rivers (vertical shapes formed by adjacent gaps), are all commonplace in justified text (below).

The first line has large white spaces opening up (a) while in contrast, the penultimate line has too little space (b). Hyphenation can fix both problems (c) by allowing words to break to give a better balance. Care needs to be taken so that words are hyphenated or broken in logical places.

A common problem with justified type is 'white acne' or 'pig bristles' – the sporadic appearance of white spaces that occur in the gaps between words. 'Rivers', or lines formed through connecting white gaps, are also to be avoided. A valuable tip for identifying problems is to look at text with squinted eyes, so you **see** only shapes and don't **read** the words; turning your text upside down also works.

type personality

We often associate personality characteristics with typefaces; for example, we say some fonts are authoritative, while others are playful. The personalities we find in typography extend to our interpretation of the message that a piece of text conveys. It also reflects the values of the person or organization that has produced it. If the atmosphere value of a font has a consistent meaning with what the words actually say, it is said to have congeniality. With poor congeniality, or inconsistency, a reader will respond slower to the text and may not accept the message. What is your reaction to the words below? Too much personality can be a bad thing and reduce legibility.

The personality of a typeface can add to the overall design effect, detract from it or have a neutral effect. To use fonts to their full advantage, an awareness of typeface personality is therefore important.

CONTEMPORARY?

Monotype Gallia
A Monotype Classic font with no accompanying lower case.

SERIOUS?

Playbill 1938 Robert Harling
Extra heavy slab serif typeface.

Pop 1992 Neville Brody
A modern typeface referencing bitmap technology — anything but traditional.

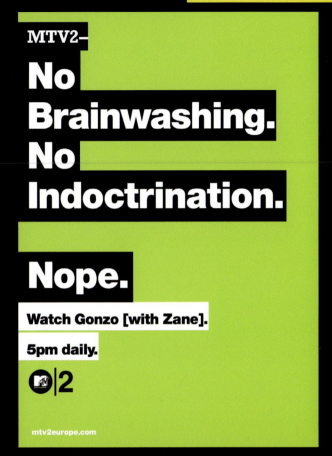

MTV2 ↑ ←

This ident rebranding uses throwaway slogans for a channel without fixed schedules or structures. It is targeted at 16–25-year-old males and sees itself as 'liquid TV'. The type personality is simple, disposable and purposefully crude to create dialogue with the audience in its own patois. The type has attitude, but doesn't take itself seriously, and because it is modular it can be easily and quickly refreshed to reflect the continuing changes of youth culture.

Design: DixonBaxi

special characters and ligatures

An alphabet alone is not enough to be able to structure textural information or communicate phonetic stresses and the infinite number of ideas and propositions that we want to. For this we need various special characters. Punctuation enables us to qualify, quantify and organize information; accents provide us with information about how a letter is stressed or sounded; and pictograms provide shorthand information, such as currency units.

The characters shown below are some of the special characters used for punctuation or to aid communication within a text.

Punctuation		"	double prime	**Accents**		**Pictograms**	
'	apostrophe	" "	double quotes	´	acute	*	asterisk
,	comma	' '	single quotes		(á, é, í, ó, ú)	¶	pilcrow
( )	parenthesis	**Points**			(á, é, í, ó, ú)	ß	eszett
{ }	braces	·	overdot	`	grave	Æ	aesc
[ ]	square brackets	·	midpoint		(à, è, ì, ò, ù)	¥	yen
-	hyphen	.	period		(à, è, ì, ò, ù)	£	sterling
–	en dash	•	bullet	¨	umlaut/dieresis	$	dollar
—	em dash				(ä, ë, ï, ö, ü)	€	euro
_	lowline/underscore	**Characters**			(ä, ë, ï, ö, ü)	@	at
:	colon	+	addition	^	circumflex	™	trademark
;	semicolon	-	subtraction		(â, ê, î, ô, û)	©	copyright
/	solidus	x	multiplication		(â, ê, î, ô, û)	&	ampersand
\	backslash	÷	division	~	tilde	†	dagger
...	ellipsis	%	per cent		(ã, ñ, õ)	‡	double dagger
! ¡	exclamation	‰	per million		(ã, ñ, õ)	§	section
¿?	question mark	#	octothorpe/hash	˘	breve	Ω	omega
>	greater than	=	equal	˛	cedilla	∞	infinity
<	less than	°	degree			☞	fist
« »	guillemets	°	ring				
'	prime						

Hyphens, en dashes and em dashes
A hyphen is typically one-third of the length of the em. The typographic use of these characters varies widely and they are often confused. A hyphen is used to separate parts of compound words, to link the words of a phrase and to connect syllables of a word that are split between separate lines. Em rules and en rules are used to delineate nested clauses in a sentence. Em rules are typically preferred in the USA, with the letters of preceding and succeeding words closed up. The en rule is typically preferred in Europe with a space either side of it.

hyphen   en dash   em dash

Knoll Christmas card   ↑

'Noël' and 'Knoll' combine to make a succinct Christmas card for the furniture manufacturer. Negative tracking is used to merge the meaning of the two words. A typographic gift; no pun intended.

Frutiger's grid

Adrian Frutiger is prominent in the pantheon of typeface designers due to the many typefaces he has created but in particular the Univers family, launched in 1957 by Deberny & Peignot.

A key reason for its success was the numbering system he developed to identify the width and weight of each of the family's 21 original cuts. There are in excess of 50 members now following revisions and extensions to this family, some of which are shown on the opposite page. His achievement with Univers is not confined to providing a wide range of typefaces.

The diagrammatic presentation of the Univers typeface family by Frutiger provides a sense of order and homogeneity through the relationships of weight and width they have with each other. This grid provided a visual key and a standard that subsequent typeface designers have been able to use to devise and shape their own families. This system has since been adopted by other type producers as can be seen with Helvetica Neue.

Helvetica
Helvetica was designed by Max Miedinger in 1957 for the Haas type foundry. It became one of the dominant typefaces of the 1960s. This typeface was formerly called Neue Haas Grotesk. It was designed with an 'anonymous' character in the modernist style.

Helvetica Neue 95
Helvetica Neue 85
Helvetica Neue 75
Helvetica Neue 65
Helvetica Neue 55
Helvetica Neue 45
Helvetica Neue 35
Helvetica Neue 25

Adrian Frutiger is an internationally renowned typographer who, as well as creating many typefaces, created house styles for various international organizations and is credited with creating the complete public signage system for the Charles de Gaulle airport in Paris.

39
Univers

45
Univers

46
Univers

47
Univers

48
Univers

49
Univers

53
Univers

55
Univers

56
Univers

57
Univers

58
Univers

59
Univers

63
Univers

65
Univers

66
Univers

67
Univers

68
Univers

73
Univers

75
Univers

76
Univers

83
Univers

Univers

Adrian Frutiger is well respected for a number of typefaces – particularly Univers. Released in 1957 by Deberny & Peignot foundry in Paris, the typeface was released in both metal and photo type.

Frutiger subsequently used this system for other typefaces: Serifa, Glypha, Frutiger, Avenir etc.

Other type manufacturers have since adopted this system as can be seen with Helvetica Neue (opposite).

83

type detailing

Typefaces vary in many ways. Some have serifs, some do not. Letterspacing is not the most obvious characteristic that springs to mind when specifying a typeface, but in certain applications it is of prime concern. Letterspacing is the space that a letter occupies – a typeface is either monospaced or proportionally spaced.

Monospaced type
Each character in a monospaced typeface occupies the same width irrespective of its actual size. These typefaces were originally used on typewriters. They enable text that lines up in vertical columns to be easily produced such as for invoices. Courier is a common monospaced typeface in the personal computer age.

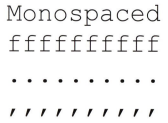

Proportionally spaced type
A system of proportional spacing was used by the Monotype and Linotype print foundries because it mimics the letter spacing of historical handset forms. Individual characters occupy a space proportional to their size.

Proportionally spaced
ffffffffffffffffffffffff

· · · · · · · · · · · · · · · · ·

, , , , , , , , , , , , , , , , , ,

Lining numerals
The majority of typefaces contain a set of lining numerals and characters that have equal height and equal, or monospaced, widths. Monospaced characters allow numerals to be vertically aligned, which is important for tabular information such as accounts, and because they are the same height they are easy to read.

2,341,536,685.00
153,687,145.18
515,598.89

Old style numerals
These are sometimes called lower-case numerals; they have different heights that can make them more difficult to read.

2,341,536,685.00

Non-aligning numerals
These characters occupy widths proportional to their size making them unsuitable for presenting tabular information.

2,341,536,685.00
153,687,145.18
515,598.89

Type sizes

Type obviously gets bigger as you increase the type size, but because typefaces have different weights some appear to be bigger than others when they are at the same point size.

Meanline

x-height

Baseline

x-height

The x-height is not a fixed measurement. It is not even related to the point size of a given typeface. All the Xs above are set in 50-point type yet some are bigger than others. The x-height is a relative measurement that refers to the distance between the baseline and the meanline.

GENERATED SMALL CAPS   TRUE SMALL CAPS

Small caps (above)

True small caps have characters that are rendered at the same weight. Small caps generated by typesetting programs are not.

Italics and obliques (below)

The italic font for some typefaces is produced by inclining the Roman font. This is really an oblique (below). A true italic, such as Palatino, is essentially a redrawn typeface (bottom). Note the difference in the letter 'a'.

Fractions (below)

Fractions can be presented in different ways. They commonly appear as unset fractions when you type the numerals on your computer (top row). Em fractions (middle row) are created using superscript and subscript numerals separated by a solidus (slash). Nut fractions are normally pre-generated within a typeface (bottom row).

Helvetica Roman
Helvetica Italic

Palatino
Palatino

1/6 3/4 1/4 3/8
Unset fractions

⅙ ¾ ¼ ⅜
Em fractions

$$\frac{1}{6} \qquad \frac{3}{4} \qquad \frac{1}{4} \qquad \frac{3}{8}$$
Nut fractions

typographic themes

Graphic design is subject to the changing intellectual and aesthetic trends that influence the work of designers and reflect the attitudes of society at large. Design responds to the changing themes that govern the way we view the world. These trends help shape the development and evolution of graphic design as a creative discipline, opening new doors of creative possibility.

Modernism

Modernism (1890–1940) through the cubist, surrealist and Dadaist movements was shaped by the industrialization and urbanization of Western society. Modernists, including the De Stijl, constructivism and Bauhaus movements, departed from the rural and provincial zeitgist prevalent in the Victorian era, rejecting its values and styles in favour of cosmopolitanism. Functionality and progress, expressed through the maxim of 'form follows function' became key concerns in the attempt to move beyond the external physical representation of reality through experimentation in a struggle to define what should be considered 'modern'. In graphic design, modernism embraced an asymmetrical approach to layout with strict adherence to the grid, an emphasis on white space and sans-serif typography, and the absence of decoration and embellishment.

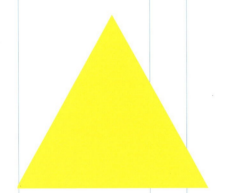

the bauhaus

the bauhaus opened in 1919 under the direction of the renowned architect walter gropius, and was intended to be a fresh approach to design after the first world war.

de stijl

an art and design movement founded around the magazine of the same name. founded by theo van doesburg, de stijl used strong rectangular forms, employed primary colours and celebrated asymmetrical compositions.

constructivism

russian constructivism was influential to modernism through its use of black and red sans-serif typography, arranged in asymmetrical blocks.

kandinsky

in 1923, kandinsky (1866–1944) proposed that there was a universal relationship between the three basic shapes and the three primary colours. the yellow triangle was the most active and dynamic, through to the passive cold blue circle.

Universal 1925 Herbert Bayer

Bayer's Universal typeface was developed at the Bauhaus and is a reduction of roman forms to simple geometric shapes. The circular form features heavily, and you can see how each character is closely based on the others.

ABCDEFGHIJKLMNOPQRSTUVWXYZ
abcdefghijklmnopqrstuvwxyz 1234567890

Kabel 1927–29 Rudolf Koch
Note the uniform nature of the characters.

ABCDEFGHIJKLMNOPQRSTUVWXYZ
abcdefghijklmnopqrstuvwxyz 1234567890

Eurostile 1962 Aldo Novarese
Letterforms are square shaped.

ABCDEFGHIJKLMNOPQRSTUVWXYZ
abcdefghijklmnopqrstuvwxyz 1234567890

Frutiger 1976 Adrian Frutiger
Again, notice the uniform nature of the characters.

ABCDEFGHIJKLMNOPQRSTUVWXYZ
abcdefghijklmnopqrstuvwxyz 1234567890

Futura 1927–30 Paul Renner
Note the straight tail of the Q and the geometric form of the G.

ABCDEFGHIJKLMNOPQRSTUVWXYZ
abcdefghijklmnopqrstuvwxyz 1234567890

Litera 1983, Michael Neugebauer
Inspired by the simple geometric shapes of early Bauhaus fonts, the clear forms of the circle, triangle and rectangle are evident.

*

'Vernacular design' used to describe 'finding' reference in the differences. An example of which is Barry Deck's Template Gothic font, based on American signage. 'The sign was done with lettering templates and it was exquisite. It had obviously been done by someone who was totally naive', explained Deck.

Arcadia 1990 Neville Brody
Brody based Arcadia on a banner he designed for Arena magazine that was itself inspired by the characters from an IBM golf ball typewriter.

Industria 1989 Neville Brody
Industria was designed for The Face magazine.

Often utilizing vernacular*
and undesigned artifacts,
postmodernism was pioneered by
the Basel School in Switzerland
and later the Cranbrook Academy
of Art in the United States.

Postmodernism Postmodernism developed following the Second World War and questioned the very notion that there is a reliable reality through deconstructing authority. It established order by engaging in the idea of fragmentation, incoherence and the plain ridiculous.

Postmodernism returned to earlier ideas of adornment and decoration, celebrating expression and personal intuition in favour of formula and structure. In typography, this saw the return of more elaborate, decorative and ornate fonts that moved away from purely functional forms.

Mrs Eaves 1996 Zuzana Licko
A revival of Baskerville. Named after Sarah Eaves, John Baskerville's housekeeper.

ABCDEFGHIJKLMNOPQRSTUVWXYZ
abcdefghijklmnopqrstuvwxyz 1234567890

Blur 1992 Neville Brody
The traditional letterforms are 'blurred' to create a new font.

ABCDEFGHIJKLMNOPQRSTUVWXYZ
abcdefghijklmnopqrstuvwxyz 1234567890

Template Gothic 1990 Barry Deck
Inspired by stencilled lettering.

ABCDEFGHIJKLMNOPQRSTUVWXYZ
abcdefghijklmnopqrstuvwxyz 1234567890

Trixie 1991 Erik van Blokland
Distressed lettering informed by the manual nature of the typewriter.

ABCDEFGHIJKLMNOPQRSTUVWXYZ
abcdefghijklmnopqrstuvwxyz 1234567890

Dot Matrix 1995 Cornel Windlin, Stephan Müller
An electronic data-signage influenced font.

ABCDEFGHiJKLMNOPQRSTUVWXYZ
abcdefghijklmnopqrstuvwxyz 1234567890

Keedy Sans 1989 Jeffery Keedy
Eclectic sans-serif font with irregular bar widths.

89

Type classification / Type in the environment

A
B
C
D
E
F
G
H
I
J

Exercise #1 – Type classification

Premise
Type can be classified in several ways according to its styling, characteristics and historical epoch. The original classification systems, it could be argued, don't relate to how we currently use typography.

Exercise
Think of a new way of classifying type that is tailored to your specific type usage needs, or specific to an area of design you are interested in. An example of this could be to classify type by how it has come to be used, for example in films, books, websites and the music industry. Alternatively, you may choose to classify it by popularity – from the most common to the least frequently seen. You may also consider classifying type by how it makes us feel, what it is reminiscent of, or how it is constructed.

Outcome
Produce a visualization of your classification and the main points that determine which category a typeface will belong to. This visualization may take the form of a poster, a piece of moving image, or a small book.

Aim
To encourage students to take a detailed look at different type characteristics and to be able to characterize them to improve communication about typefaces.

Fonts ↑ ←

Different fonts have different characteristics and personalities. Some are formal, others fun, some have a distinct 'style' while others are discreet. Familiarizing yourself with different fonts will enable considered and appropriate type selection.

Exercise #2 – Type in the environment

Premise
The urban environment is full of typography set in different typefaces, colours, point sizes and utilizing various interpretations of typographical conventions.

Exercise
Photograph various examples of typography from the urban environment within different settings and locations, including handmade signs.

Outcome
Report on your findings on how type is used in the environment and what surprised you about this found typography.

Aim
To encourage the student to explore how different typographic styles are used in different contexts and settings.

Signage   ←   ↓

Type in the environment takes myriad forms, such as the 'visitor parking' and 'no diving' signs here, that can stimulate and inspire designers through the chance encounter with different presentations and usages.

PORNO-GRAPHY NEEDS ↓YOU↓

Image

Image refers to the pictorial graphic elements that can bring a design alive. Whether as the main focus of a page or a subsidiary element, images play an essential role in communicating a message and are a key part of establishing the visual feel of a piece of work. Images perform a number of functions, from conveying the drama of a news report to summing up and supporting an argument presented in the copy, or providing a visual break to an expanse of text. Images are effective because they instantly communicate an idea or a feeling that the reader can comprehend quickly. For instance, how would you describe the latest fashion trend in words? This is difficult compared to the relative ease of showing it in a picture.

Image use includes working with different types of pictures (such as illustration and photography), how we talk about images (for example, what is an icon or a pictogram), and the pragmatic considerations for image usage (such as resolution and getting it to print or display as intended).

Fuse ←

Through Fuse magazine – founded by Neville Brody and Jon Wozencroft – typography exploded into uncharted realms as type designers grabbed hold of the 'free reins' that computer technology put in their hands. Fuse features expressive type generation where the symbolism of type stepped to the fore and gained the upper hand over mere functionality, addressing societal issues through the shapes and style of the letters. Each issue of Fuse came with a disk of new typefaces. Opposite is the 1994 poster by Fuel that features the font F Tape Type, which combines type and image.

Design: Neville Brody / Research Studios

image meaning

Images are powerful communicators because of the emotional, cultural and factual meanings that we read into their content. How images are presented also affects how their messages are received as, they can have both cognitive and denotive meanings. Something signified by a visible sign is a denotive meaning. For example, 'house' is a denotive that we associate with a building, but it also has secondary cognitive meanings. Cognition refers to things that we have perceived, learned and reasoned. A picture of a house denotes a home, or the place where you live, but it also has other connotations, such as family and security.

Semiotics

Semiotics is the study of signs and offers explanations as to how we interpret images. Semiotics says that a given image can communicate meaning in three ways: the sign or what it shows, the larger system that this is part of and the context within which it is presented. As designers, we need to be aware of these facets because what we intend to convey using images and signs isn't always interpreted as we intended.

The signifier and the signified

A signifier communicates information about an object. For example, a word is a signifier, or a series of letters or shapes, that we know have a meaning. The signified is the object or idea that the signifier is communicating. For example, the letters H O U S E form the word house, and signify a building or home. When the two elements combine, the result is a sign. There are three main types of sign as shown below.

Symbol

Symbols speak to us through what they represent rather than what they actually are. The symbols above represent man and woman although they look nothing like a man or a woman. However, they are powerful communicators or signifiers of this information.

Icon

An icon is a graphic element that represents an object, person or something else. It is typically a reduction of an object such that it is instantly recognizable for what it is. These icons represent man and woman and are a simplified silhouette of a man and woman.

Index

An index is a symbol that creates a link between the object and the sign. For example, this shoe symbol could be an index for woman because it is clearly recognizable as a female and feminine shoe.

THE INDEX OF POSSIBILITIES WITHIN A MORE OPEN COMMUNICATION IS DETERMINED NOT BY A MONOLOGUE, BUT IN THE ACCEPTANCE THAT INTERVENTIONS MADE BY DESIGN CAN ACT AS A MEDIATING INFLUENCE AND ARE PART OF A LARGER REFLEXIVE PROCESS.
THE PROJECT AIMS TO EXPLORE OUR COLLECTIVE UNDERSTANDING OF THE PROCESSES AND RESPONSIBILITIES WITHIN GRAPHIC DESIGN, ITS RELATIONSHIP TO COMMUNICATION AND LANGUAGE, AND IMPORTANTLY THE INTENTION ON THE PART OF THE MAKER OR DESIGNER.

IMAGETRAP

WE INTERRUPT THE PROGRAMME IS AN INVESTIGATION NOT ONLY INTO THE DIALOGIC PRODUCTION OF MESSAGES AND THE MAPPING OF SHARED EXPERIENCE, BUT ALSO THE WAY IN WHICH IT IS POSSIBLE TO SEE GRAPHIC DESIGN AS A FORM OF SOCIAL COMMENTARY.

INHERENT WITHIN THE COMMUNICATION PROCESS MUST BE A CONSIDERATION OF THE NEGOTIATED INTERPRETATION THAT OCCURS IN THE UNDERSTANDING OF MESSAGES.
WE INTERRUPT THE PROGRAMME IS AN ATTEMPT TO EXPLORE THE NATURE OF GRAPHIC DESIGN AS A DIRECT COMPONENT OF THE COMMUNICATION PROCESS. THIS COLLABORATIVE PROJECT INVESTIGATES THE USE OF THE MEDIUM IN A MORE DEMOCRATIC, OPEN FASHION, WHERE ALL PARTICIPANTS HAVE A GENUINE INVESTMENT IN THE EXPERIENCE OF A MESSAGE.

LANGUAGE

BY CHALLENGING THE DETERMINIST MODEL OF COMMUNICATION, THE PROJECT SETS UP THE CONDITIONS BY WHICH THE FORMULATION OF A PARTNERSHIP IN THE CONSTRUCTION OF MEANING (BETWEEN PRIMARY AND SECONDARY MAKERS AND READERS) MAY BE FURTHER CONSIDERED.

Independent
Magazine

Can Britain bite back?

Independent
Magazine

Sisters to the death

languageimagetrap ↑

These posters for a design and education research project feature juxtapositions of a contemporary image with details from an old painting. A solitary word across each poster combines with the image providing a clue to the lecture's content, questioning how image and language relate. The reader applies a cognitive meaning from the association of the word and the image.

Design: Visual Research

Independent Magazine ←

This magazine cover abandons straplines for an image-based page

image types

There are two main types of digital image – rasters and vectors. They refer to how images are generated, saved and used. Each image type has particular advantages and disadvantages and can be manipulated and used in different ways.

Rasters

A raster or bitmap image is any graphic image that is composed of picture elements or pixels in a grid where each pixel contains colour information for the image. Bitmap graphics are generally not scalable because they have a fixed resolution, which means that when you resize them the image can become distorted and have a jagged, pixellated edge. Rasters are images made of pixels, which only reproduce correctly at a certain size. Any enlargement will cause a decrease in quality. The image below is at 300 dpi at 100%, and to the right is a lower resolution 72 dpi image enlarged to the same size showing the degradation in quality.

Vectors

A vector image is made up of many individual, scalable objects that are defined by mathematical formulae rather than pixels, which makes them scalable or resolution independent. Fonts, for example, are vector objects. The main disadvantage of vector images is that they are unsuitable for reproducing photo-realistic images because they cannot depict the continuous subtle tones of a photograph. As vectors are a mathematical process, they are scalable and can be enlarged infinitely without loss of quality or resolution. The 1,000% enlargement of a section of a poster on the following page demonstrates the clarity of type and line at such magnification.

 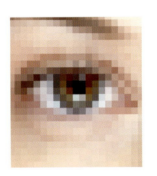  

Image resolution and file formats

Understanding some of the mechanics of how raster images work can help a designer achieve good results from them. The spacing of the pixels in an image determine its resolution. The resolution of an image is measured in pixels per inch (ppi), which is also called dots per inch (dpi). The higher the resolution of an image, the more pixels or information it will contain. A higher resolution means an image contains more detail and so more colour transitions or tones can be recorded. At low resolutions, an image may not contain sufficient information to conserve or record detail, which is why low-resolution images often contain areas that are pixellated. This often happens when an image is enlarged because the number of pixels in an image is fixed, so its resolution decreases as it is enlarged.

It is important to bear in mind where an image will be used in order to work with an appropriate resolution. For example, monitors have 72 dpi resolution, which is why web graphics are produced at this low resolution. Low resolution also makes them quicker to download. Printing processes often require a minimum 300 dpi resolution, while high-end image setters can print at 1,200 dpi, 2,400 dpi or more.

JERWOOD APPLIED ARTS PRIZE 2002 TEXTILES

CRAFTS COUNCIL

Jerwood Applied Arts   ←   ↑

This is the outer cover for the Jerwood Applied Arts Prize Textiles catalogue. A single row of pixels is elongated to create an abstract image. The ambiguity of the resulting graphic is used as an overall identity to the collection, rather than focusing on a single piece of work.

Design: NB: Studio

DPI, LPI and PPI

<u>DPI</u> (dots per inch) is a measurement that refers to how many ink dots a printer can deposit within an inch. A resolution of 300 dpi is standard amongst the printing industry, although this will vary depending on the print job quality required. Large-format jobs, such as bill posters, are often printed at a lower resolution, while glossy fashion magazines are often printed at higher resolutions. It must be noted that the default screen resolution is 72 dpi even for images that have higher resolutions. This means that a 300-dpi image will still be displayed at 72 dpi on the monitor.

<u>LPI</u> (lines per inch) is a measurement that refers to how printers reproduce photographic images. Photographs are reproduced as a series of halftone dots of different sizes. The larger the dots, the darker the image produced and vice versa. A printer uses a half-tone grid to produce the half-tone dots. The grid is divided into cells and LPI is a measurement of how close these cells are to each other. A low LPI value means there are fewer cells and the half-tone dots will be more obvious in the printed image.

<u>PPI</u> (pixels per inch) is a measurement of the number of pixels displayed in an image.

Knoll

Twenty-First
Century Classics

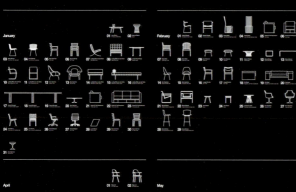

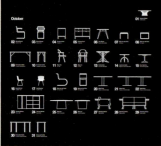

Knoll ← ↑

These posters feature the use of line art images produced as vectors to show various different chair styles produced by Knoll. The line art set against a plain colour background focuses the viewers' attention on the graceful lines of the furniture without the distraction of a room setting. Vectors are scalable and this means that the design could be produced easily at different scales, such as posters and postcards, without suffering any image degradation.

Design: NB: Studio

Synthesizers ← ↑

These synthesizer-inspired posters show how they have influenced the evolution of music in the past few decades. The artwork of the synthesizers was produced as vectors so that they could be easily scaled and adjusted.

Design: Dorian Design

altering images

Images can be altered or enhanced in different ways to recast, contextualize or refresh the information they contain. Techniques such as collage, juxtaposition and the use of graphic effects can dramatically alter an image and give it new meaning.

Most images are now taken and stored digitally, which means that they can easily be subject to many changes, alterations or enhancements. More graphic effects and filters can also be applied.

Filters
Whether attached to a camera lens or an adjustment in a photo-editing computer program, filters allow changes to be made to an image. Filters make adjustments to the information an image contains. They may produce subtle changes, such as refining a colour image to create an opal blue sky for a coral sand beach. They are also used to make more dramatic graphic interventions, such as the glowing edges filter used on the diver below.

Channels and levels
Changing the channels and levels settings of an image will alter its hue and brightness. The examples opposite show some of the many treatments that can be given to change the appearance of an image.

Colour balance, brightness and contrast
The levels control in photo editing software is used to change the brightness of an image – how light or dark it is. The curves control can be used to adjust the contrast of the image tones. These processes can also adjust colour balance, and the colour balance control allows for fine-tuning.

Hulton Archive   ↓   →

These images were produced for a photo library catalogue to showcase their creative potential and lead viewers away from the preconception that the company only supplies black-and-white photography. Colour and photo manipulation techniques combine to create a series of striking images that indicate some of the 'colour' possibilities for the use of black-and-white photography.

Design: Gavin Ambrose

Original image

Levels and filters create striking results

Original image

Sections of image, selected by colour values are isolated and removed

Original image

Solarized version

Original image

Levels adjusted to remove
background noise, converted to
bitmap and filled

Screened shapes overlay the
original image

Image of Frida Kahlo adjusted to
look painterly

Channels moved out of registration
to overlap one another, mimicking
a 3-D effect

Greyscale colour halftone
giving the illusion of newsprint
image quality

Duotone of red and black with the
value of red set to full

Colour channels moved out of
registration to overlap, and the top
layer coloured

Full-colour image in half-tone

Further channel adjustment

101

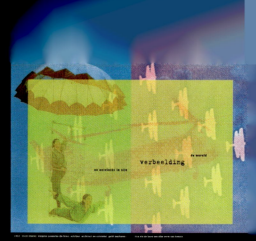

Z[00] Agenda ← ↑

These striking images were inspired by the random imagery of the everyday world including graffiti, print, imperfect photos, signage, odd ephemera, textures and architecture. They are composed of individual elements that form rough visual blocks enhanced by hand-drawn elements, layer blending, colour filtering and found elements.

Design: Faydherbe / de Vringer

Collage ↓

The collection below is a collage of found elements including paint charts, newspapers, chewing gum wrappers, old sepia photographs and photographic elements that have been cut out.

Design: Craig Yamey

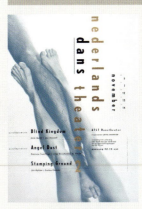

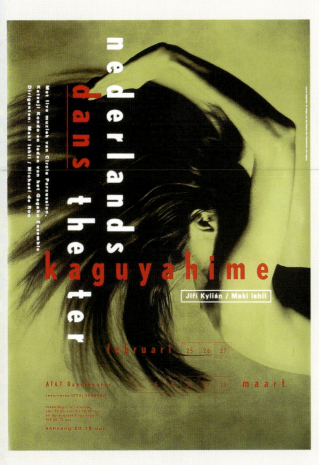

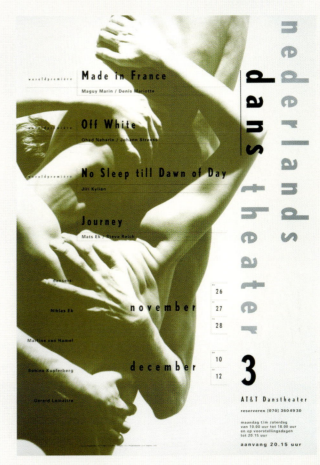

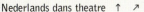

Nederlands dans theatre ↑ ↗

These posters feature coloured duotone images of dancers that are close cropped to capture the drama and movement of dance. The tonality of the images has been reduced to enhance contrast and highlight the sculptural effects of the bodies. This high contrast has been achieved by removing the grey or midtones to leave the black-and-white tones.

Design: Faydherbe / de Vringer

Image manipulation

Image manipulation in the days before computers was an arcane alchemical art practised in darkrooms or with an airbrush. Technology has relocated this role to graphic designers and armed them with a vast array of software tools and effects, and the hardware to power them. The only limits are the creative abilities of the user.

The many possibilities of image manipulation include: photo retouching, colouring, overlaying of images, superimposing of elements, cut outs, shape alteration and blending. Rather than provide an exhaustive and marginally useful list of techniques, the following examples of imaginative image manipulation will give some idea of just how broad the possibilities are.

Requiem for a Dream   ↑

Type and image are superimposed upon each other to create a visually arresting poster.

Design: NB: Studio

Odd ephemera   ↑   ↗   →

These striking images were inspired by the random imagery of the everyday world including graffiti, print, imperfect photos, signage, odd ephemera, textures and architecture. They are composed of individual elements that form rough visual blocks enhanced by hand-drawn elements, layer blending, colour filtering and found elements.

Design: Andy Potts

type as image

So far, we have addressed type primarily in relation to its principal function: using letters to communicate words. Type can also be used as a symbol or icon that speaks more through its visual representation than the meanings of the constituent letters, although, of course, the fact that the letters may mean something gives an added significance to such an image. Logos are a common example of this. How do we associate a logo with a company? Is it through its visual statement or the letters that comprise it?

Joe Kerr ↑

This business card for architectural historian Joe Kerr has transformed a rather unimaginative piece of graffiti on a bollard into a fun, slightly irreverent and unique piece of identity. The linkage works for the simple reason that the business card is for someone named Joe (we can assume that he didn't graffiti the post in order to take the photo).

Design: Studio Myerscough

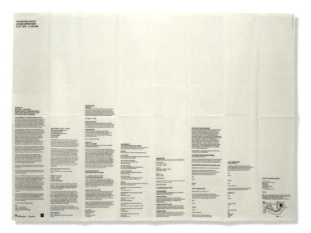

4th Estate ←

Frost Design keeps things simple (left) with its work for the 4th Estate catalogue. The use of typography is sacrificed for a more natural, back-to-basics, handwritten lettering. NYC is a dramatic statement in itself and pushed to the extreme by the designer. The lack of information on one side of the poster is countered by the reverse side, where text columns are reminiscent of New York's skyscrapers and skyline.

Design: Frost Design

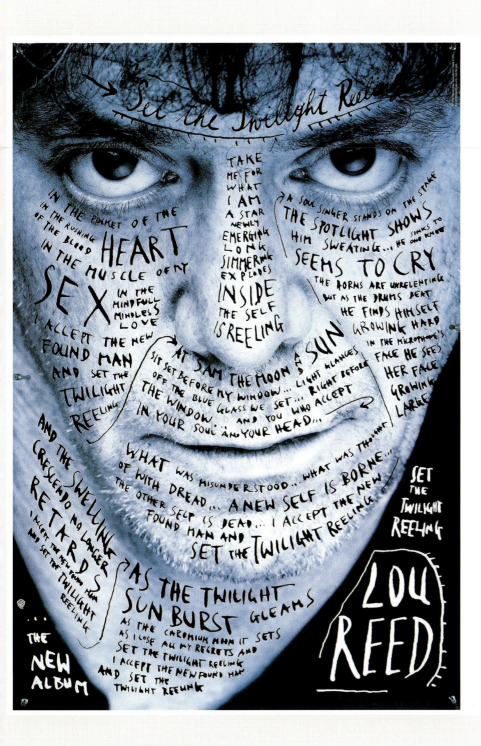

Lou Reed ←

The songs on Lou Reed's album, Set the Twilight Reeling, have extremely personal lyrics. The design studio took the lyrics as the starting point for the design of the album's cover by writing the words directly over the artist's face. The handwritten script, tailored to the contours of his face, adds to the impression of intimacy and almost looks as though it has been tattooed, so that Lou Reed bares his soul visually as well as aurally.

Design: Sagmeister Inc

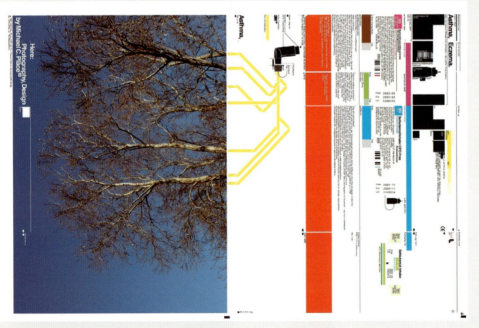

Build ← ↑

These designs by Michael C Place, founder of Build, feature a mixture of simplicity and complexity that explores the design medium. The designs use the elements of text, colour and image set in non-traditional ways to create multiple layers of information that interact in an intriguing way, which pulls the viewer into the designs.

Design: Build

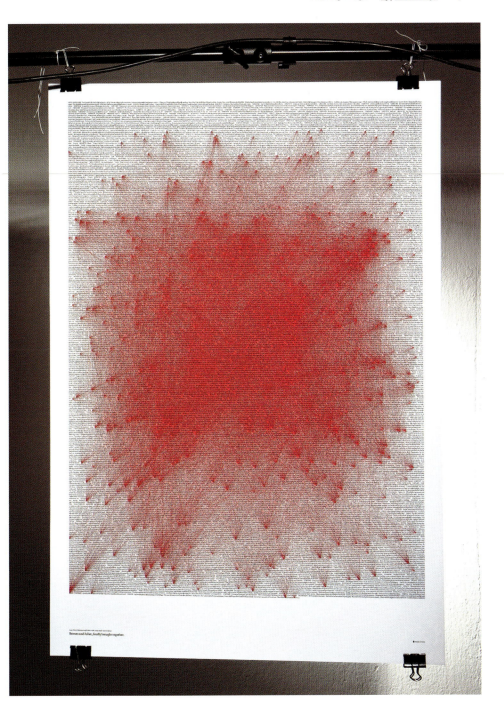

Romeo and Juliet ↑ ←

This large-format poster features text from Shakespeare's play, Romeo and Juliet, within which the word 'Juliet' appears 180 times and the word Romeo 308 times. The couple were finally united by 55,440 red lines. The large format allowed the designers to include all the text on a single folio.

Design: Beetroot

layers

Images can be created with several different layers where each layer contains specific elements of information that together form the resulting image. The use of layers to separate the different component parts of an image allows for the easy manipulation of each one, independent of the other layers.

Using layers

Layers allow a designer to keep order when manipulating different parts of an image. Each type of manipulation should occur on a new layer. Image manipulation software contains different overlays that produce different image effects.

Composite images

Using layers results in a large file size. Once the image is finalized, a composite is produced that becomes a single layer with a smaller file size that is easier to use and share. The original image will normally be a PSD file, while the composite will be a JPEG file.

Botanica ←

This logo uses a simple form of layering. Different layers of leaves are used, one on top of another, with layer transparency that allows the leaves on the layers below to show through. The overall map pattern is constructed of around 70 single images.

Design: Gavin Ambrose / Adrian Sharman

BotanicaReinterpretingNature

Adjustment layers

Adjustment layers allow different original images to be combined into a single final image.

Original images
Two original raster images are selected that will be combined for graphic effect. The adjustment layer preserves the integrity of each original image.

Combining images
The amount of each image that shows in the final image can be controlled so that each is as clear and recognizable as necessary.

Combining images and effects
In this case a 'gradient map' has been applied for graphic effect.

Overlaying images
A single original image can be used several times in the final image. Here, it is reversed on a new layer to create a mirror image.

Applying filters
Different filters can be applied to change the image. Here, a solarize filter has been used.

*The Forest Stewardship Council (FSC) is an independent, non-governmental, not-for-profit organisation established to promote the responsible management of the world's forests. FSC certified forests — covering over 100 million hectares in 79 different countries — are managed to ensure long term timber supplies while protecting the environment and the lives of forest-dependent peoples. FSC accreditation is awarded to manufacturers and other users of timber-based products who demonstrate a Chain of Custody that tracks responsible use right through the supply chain to the consumer.

Intro   As an FSC* accredited printer, Team is committed to promoting the use of FSC/recycled paper and board. In line with this commitment, Team have assembled a special collection of FSC/recycled stocks available in a range of weights and finishes to cover most everyday printing requirements. These gloss, silk and uncoated stocks are offered as standard on all appropriate projects unless other branded papers are specified by the client.

This book brings together samples of all these papers and provides a useful reference guide for specifiers in selecting the most appropriate finish and weight for each project. Their quality and performance stands comparison with any other paper and because they are used by Team as standard stocks, there is virtually no cost implication against non-FSC certified paper.

Use of these papers gives added environmental credibility to the communication itself. As an FSC accredited printer using FSC certified paper, work produced by Team has the opportunity to carry a logo confirming its environmental integrity (positional logo artwork available from Team upon request). This is an important asset for all clients whose environmental policies embrace both their own communications and the activities of their suppliers.

Print matters   ↑   →

This promotional brochure for leading national printing specialist, Team, uses a series of delicate gradient and image tints. The content of the brochure focuses on the environmental impact of printing, and exemplifies the printing capabilities on these FSC and recycled stocks. The Forest Stewardship Council promotes the sustainable management of forests for use in printing and packaging.

Design: Design Project

Recycled
FSC
Silk

350/gsm

Recycled FSC Uncoated
100% recycled fibre
6 weights

Recycled
FSC
Uncoated
100/gsm

FSC
Gloss

150/gsm

Juxtaposition / Symbols and icons

Exercise #1 – Juxtaposition

Premise
Images can be powerful communicators due to the denotive and cognitive meanings they contain.

Exercise
Select an image or photograph and juxtapose it with other images to see how different denotive and cognitive meanings can be created.

Outcome
Produce a visualization of your findings that identifies the different meanings achieved by the juxtaposition of different secondary images.

Aim
To encourage a more considered appreciation of the use of image in design that goes beyond the obvious and readily available.

Relationships ↓

The placement of images in close proximity to one another establishes a relationship between them, which may be obvious or less so, based on a profound link or something more superficial. For example, the connection between the images below could be that both subjects have their mouths open.

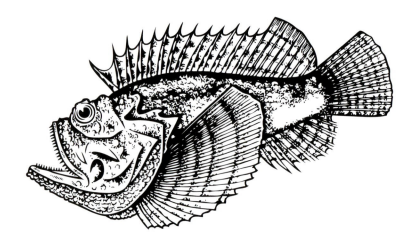

Exercise #2 – Symbols and icons

Premise
Symbols and icons provide a visual shortcut that results in the rapid communication and understanding of a piece of information.

Exercise
Find photographs that communicate three different ideas or concepts and from these, identify the key communication elements that convey them. Use the distilled elements identified as raw material with which to produce three different icons or symbols to represent each idea or concept. Consider how the use of colour may or may not help with this.

Outcome
Produce a visualization that shows your base images with the icons and symbols you have created to represent them; consider how adequately and quickly they communicate the idea or concept in the base image.

Aim
To encourage a more considered appreciation of the power of icons and symbols, and to understand how the reductive process is pared back to its visual essence through an idea or concept.

Symbols   ↑

Symbols and icons are graphic devices that communicate fundamental elements with precision.

BRITAIN

TATE

DAYS LIKE THESE Tate Triennial Exhibition of Contemporary British Art 2003

Admission free
26 February – 26 May

Tate Britain
London SW1
⊖ Pimlico
www.tate.org.uk

Colour

Colour has become a permanent fixture in the field of visual communication as four-colour printing has become ubiquitous for magazines and newspapers. Affordable personal computer printing technology means that most companies now have the capability to produce colour documents in-house. Colour adds dynamism to a design; it attracts attention and can elicit emotional responses. It can help organize the elements on a page – zoning or grouping items of a similar nature, coding certain types of information, and aiding the viewer in finding the information they require.

With colour so freely available, discipline in its use is necessary for designs to be cogent and readable. Colour usage should enhance a design's ability to communicate, adding hierarchy and pace.

Days like these   ←

This very colourful poster uses vibrant and eye-catching lines of colour. It continues on a tradition of posters inspired by Harry Beck's iconic London Underground map.

Design: NB: Studio

understanding colour

Colour is such a powerful communicator because it presents various encoded meanings, while also adding a certain dynamism. Colour can represent different states of emotion or moods and can be used to elicit a particular emotional reaction in the viewer. It can also refer to specific categories of products or concepts. It is important to note that colour meanings are culturally specific and vary across countries and cultures – as can be seen on the page opposite.

Boy

Girl

Pastel hues of blue and pink are associated with newborn children in Western cultures – pale blue for boys and pale pink for girls. This scheme is particularly used for clothing as addressed in this coding; the colours help to identify the sex of the infant.

This association is so strong that when the colours and genders are switched there is a cognitive breakdown and something appears odd, wrong or even unacceptable. A similar reaction can be expected in other cultures and parts of the world if their colour usage associations are not considered.

The ability of colour to provide instant communication and recognition plays a major role in branding and not just for products as these two pictures illustrate. New York City is known as the Big Apple, but its yellow taxi cabs are ubiquitous and easily recognizable symbols of the city.

London has its black taxi cabs, of course, but perhaps a more recognizable symbol of the city is the red telephone box. The strength of this symbolic association is highlighted by the fact that it is still made even though most red telephone boxes were withdrawn and replaced several years ago.

colour for the
n faith

Red
Used in activities in China ranging from weddings to funerals as it represents celebration and luck

Orange
Used to represent Halloween in the USA

Blue
The Chinese link blue with immortality

Brown
In Colombia this is a colour that discourages sales

olour of
ing in India

Purple
The colour of royalty in European cultures

Black
Used for mourning in Western cultures; associated with death, but also ultra cool, stylish and elegant

Green
A man wearing a green hat in China could indicate that his wife is being unfaithful

White
The colour for purity in Western cultures; used for wedding dresses

w
sents happiness
y in the West

Blue
A colour associated with protection in the Middle East; a 'safe' colour throughout the world

Yellow
A sacred and imperial colour in many Asian cultures

White
A mourning colour in Eastern cultures. It also symbolizes death

Red
When used with white in Eastern cultures it means joy

olic of loneliness
absence of love
stern societies

Blue
A sacred colour to Hindus as it is the colour of Krishna

Saffron
A sacred colour for the Hindu faith

Orange
Associated with the Protestant faith in Ireland

Green
Has negative connotations in France; also a poor choice for packaging

iated with death
an, particularly
carnations

Green
Of high significance in Muslim countries because it is the colour of Islam

Red
Can mean 'stop' or 'danger' in Western cultures; also associated with Valentine's day and Christmas

Blue
Connected to soap in Colombia

Red
Used for wedding dresses in India as it is the colour of purity

Zumtobel AG ↓ ↑

How do you demonstrate light in a printed book? This annual report for a lighting company has a vacuum-formed outer cover (shown below left), that has been photographed under different lighting conditions, demonstrating the dramatic effect lighting can have. Notice how different the image appears if cast with warm orange light, compared to the graphic, almost metallic effect achieved bottom right. This simple device shows how a creative approach to a design problem can produce dramatic effects.

Design: Sagmeister Inc

STOP ↙ ↓

This installation was part of the STOP – Instructions, Directions and Other Cases exhibition at Galerija Nova in Belgrade. The exhibition addresses the influence of mass communication on the individual and their perception of life in the contemporary world. The pieces use a visual language of commands, instructions, graphic satire and humour. The works pictured feature the use of a cool and calming cyan-blue that unifies the statements.

Design: Slavimir Stojanovic Communis DDB

basic terminology

Using and communicating about colour effectively requires an understanding of colour terminology. The following spreads explain basic colour terminology as used by designers, photographers, artists, printers and other professionals in order to communicate colour ideas.

Primary colours

Primary colours are those that can be combined to make a range of colours. Colour reproduction is based on the principles behind the three-colour (trichromatic) vision of the human eye, which contains receptors that are each sensitive to one of the additive primary colours of light: red, green and blue. Designers also need to be familiar with the subtractive primaries – cyan, magenta and yellow – that are used to reproduce the additive primaries in the four-colour printing process.

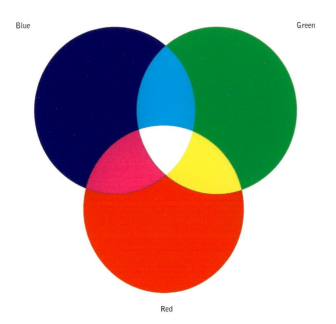

Blue Green

Red

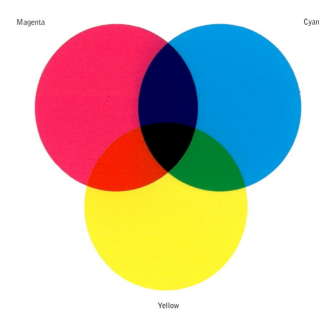

Magenta Cyan

Yellow

Additive primaries

White light is made up of red, green and blue light – the additive primaries. When only two additive primaries are combined, they create one of the subtractive primaries.

Subtractive primaries

Subtractive primaries work in the same way, but when two are combined they make an additive primary; when all are combined they produce black. These are the primaries used in the four-colour printing process to reproduce the additive primaries.

Secondary colours

A secondary colour is produced from any two primary colours used in equal proportions. In the subtractive colour space, the secondary colours are red, green and blue (the additive primaries).

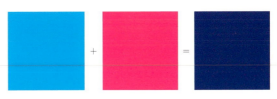

As an example, the additive primaries blue and red produce the subtractive primary magenta.

Equally, the subtractive primaries cyan and magenta produce the additive primary blue.

Tertiary colours

Tertiary colours have equal mixtures or strengths of a primary colour and the adjacent secondary colour on the colour wheel. They are equivalent to mixing two primary colours in the proportions 2:1 or 1:2. This ratio gives a strong hue and is normal when mixing printing inks. There are six tertiary colours: red-orange, yellow-orange, yellow-green, blue-green, blue-violet and red-violet.

The primary yellow and secondary dark green combine to make a tertiary light green.

The secondary cyan and secondary dark green combine to make the tertiary blue-green.

Colour assimilation

The primary, secondary and tertiary colours can be mixed within the four-colour printing process to produce a wide gamut or range of colours, as shown in the chips below. The subtractive primaries – cyan, magenta and yellow – are used in different percentage amounts to reproduce or assimilate the additive primaries (middle) and the tertiary colours (right).

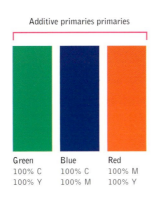

Subtractive primaries

Cyan
100% C

Magenta
100% M

Yellow
100% Y

Additive primaries primaries

Green
100% C
100% Y

Blue
100% C
100% M

Red
100% M
100% Y

Tertiary colours

Red-violet
100% M
50% C

Red-orange
100% M
50% Y

Yellow-orange
100% Y
50% M

Yellow-green
100% Y
50% M

Blue-green
100% Y
50% M

Blue-violet
100% C
50% M

Controlling hue, brightness and saturation

A designer can control and change the hue, brightness and saturation of an image to alter and improve its appearance, so that it will reproduce well in the printing process or on screen. The diagram opposite shows the results of different combinations of hue and saturation for the central image at a middle brightness level.

minimum hue　　　　　　　　　　　　　　　　　　　　　　**maximum hue**

As hue refers to the actual colours of the image, changing the hue value dramatically changes the colours of the image.

Hue (or colour)

Hue is the actual colour of an image or object. Green, red, wine and silver are all hues. Altering a hue changes the colour of a design element, but leaves the saturation and brightness at their original levels.

minimum value　　　　　　　　　　　　　　　　　　　　　**maximum value**

Adjusting the brightness level alters how much light is used to produce the colour. The more light used, the brighter the colour will be.

Value (or brightness)

Value refers to the intensity or brightness of a hue. It can be changed by mixing the hue with different amounts of black or white. The gradation above has a constant hue (black) but it changes in value from a white mix (left) to a black mix (right). The hue and saturation remain unchanged, but the image appears faded or masked with high or low levels of brightness.

minimum saturation　　　　　　　　　　　　　　　　　　**maximum saturation**

Adjusting saturation affects how vivid a colour appears. A fully saturated image contains full colour values. A desaturated image appears grey as colour vivacity is reduced.

Saturation (or chroma)

Saturation refers to the chromatic purity of a colour and the amount of grey that it contains. At maximum chroma (or saturation) a colour contains no grey. Such colours are described as vivid, bright, rich and full. At lower saturation levels, the colours contain increasing amounts of grey, which results in subdued, muted and dull colours.

Minimum hue and
maximum saturation

Maximum hue and
maximum saturation

increased saturation

decreased hue

increased hue

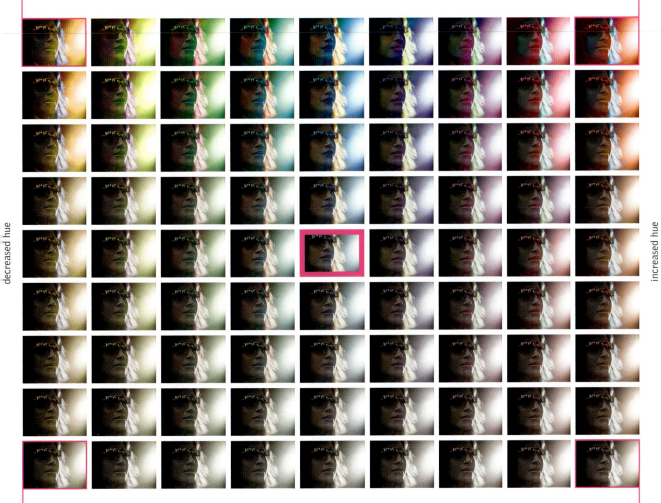

decreased saturation

Minimum hue and
minimum saturation

Maximum hue and
minimum saturation

Warm

Red-orange
Tertiary

Red
Secondary

Yellow-orange
Tertiary

Red-orange
Primary

Yellow
Primary

Red-purple
Tertiary

Yellow-green
Tertiary

Blue
Secondary

Green
Secondary

Blue-purple
Tertiary

Cyan
Secondary

Blue-green
Tertiary

Cool

The colour wheel

The colour wheel is a tool that designers use to provide guidance for colour scheme selections. The wheel is the colour spectrum formed into a circle to visually explain colour theory, such as how the primaries can interact to create secondary and tertiary colours. Colours can be described as warm or cool. There are deep-rooted associations with the colours red, orange and yellow, which can remind us of fire, the sun and warmth; cooler shades remind us of water, nature (earth and foliage), the sea and the night sky.

Colour wheel combinations

The colour wheel can be used to create a harmonious palette for a design by selecting colour combinations that work well together. Various methods can be used to select a colour palette, depending upon the number of colours required, as shown below.

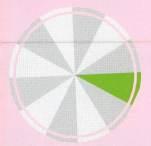

Monochrome
A monochrome colour is any single colour from the colour wheel.

Complementary
Complementary or contrasting colours are those colours that face each other on opposite sides of the colour wheel. Complementary colours have strong contrast and so result in a more vibrant design.

Split complements
Split complementary colours comprise three colours. The splits are the two colours adjacent to the complementary colour of the one that you have selected as the principal colour.

Triads
Triad colours are any three equidistant colours on the colour wheel. As all three colours contrast, a triad colour scheme provides tension to the viewer. The primary and secondary colour spaces are both triads.

Analogous
Analogous colours are the two colours on either side of a chosen colour, that is, any three consecutive colour segments on the colour wheel. Analogous colour schemes provide a harmonious, natural blend of colours.

Mutual complements
Mutual complements are a set of colours that comprise a triad of equidistant colours and the complementary colour of the central one of them.

Near complements
A near complementary colour is one that is adjacent to the colour that is a complementary colour to the principal colour.

Double complements
Double complements are any two adjacent colours and their two complements on the opposite side of the colour wheel.

Name	Hex Code RGB	Decimal Code
IndianRed	CD 5C 5C	205 92 92
LightCoral	F0 80 80	240 128 128
Salmon	FA 80 72	250 128 114
DarkSalmon	E9 96 7A	233 150 122
LightSalmon	FF A0 7A	255 160 122
Crimson	DC 14 3C	220 20 60
Red	FF 00 00	255 0 0
FireBrick	B2 22 22	178 34 34
DarkRed	8B 00 00	139 0 0
Pink	FF C0 CB	255 192 203
LightPink	FF B6 C1	255 182 193
HotPink	FF 69 B4	255 105 180
DeepPink	FF 14 93	255 20 147
MediumVioletRed	C7 15 85	199 21 133
PaleVioletRed	DB 70 93	219 112 147
LightSalmon	FF A0 7A	255 160 122
Coral	FF 7F 50	255 127 80
Tomato	FF 63 47	255 99 71
OrangeRed	FF 45 00	255 69 0
DarkOrange	FF 8C 00	255 140 0
Orange	FF A5 00	255 165 0
Gold	FF D7 00	255 215 0
Yellow	FF FF 00	255 255 0
LightYellow	FF FF E0	255 255 224
LemonChiffon	FF FA CD	255 250 205
LightGoldenrodYellow	FA FA D2	250 250 210
PapayaWhip	FF EF D5	255 239 213
Moccasin	FF E4 B5	255 228 181
PeachPuff	FF DA B9	255 218 185
PaleGoldenrod	EE E8 AA	238 232 170
Khaki	F0 E6 8C	240 230 140
DarkKhaki	BD B7 6B	189 183 107
Lavender	E6 E6 FA	230 230 250
Thistle	D8 BF D8	216 191 216
Plum	DD A0 DD	221 160 221
Violet	EE 82 EE	238 130 238
Orchid	DA 70 D6	218 112 214
Fuchsia	FF 00 FF	255 0 255
Magenta	FF 00 FF	255 0 255
MediumOrchid	BA 55 D3	186 85 211
MediumPurple	93 70 DB	147 112 219
Amethyst	99 66 CC	153 102 204
BlueViolet	8A 2B E2	138 43 226
DarkViolet	94 00 D3	148 0 211
DarkOrchid	99 32 CC	153 50 204
DarkMagenta	8B 00 8B	139 0 139
Purple	80 00 80	128 0 128

Name	Hex Code RGB	Decimal Code
Indigo	4B 00 82	75 0 130
SlateBlue	6A 5A CD	106 90 205
DarkSlateBlue	48 3D 8B	72 61 139
MediumSlateBlue	7B 68 EE	123 104 238
GreenYellow	AD FF 2F	173 255 47
Chartreuse	7F FF 00	127 255 0
LawnGreen	7C FC 00	124 252 0
Lime	00 FF 00	0 255 0
LimeGreen	32 CD 32	50 205 50
PaleGreen	98 FB 98	152 251 152
LightGreen	90 EE 90	144 238 144
MediumSpringGreen	00 FA 9A	0 250 154
SpringGreen	00 FF 7F	0 255 127
MediumSeaGreen	3C B3 71	60 179 113
SeaGreen	2E 8B 57	46 139 87
ForestGreen	22 8B 22	34 139 34
Green	00 80 00	0 128 0
DarkGreen	00 64 00	0 100 0
YellowGreen	9A CD 32	154 205 50
OliveDrab	6B 8E 23	107 142 35
Olive	80 80 00	128 128 0
DarkOliveGreen	55 6B 2F	85 107 47
MediumAquamarine	66 CD AA	102 205 170
DarkSeaGreen	8F BC 8F	143 188 143
LightSeaGreen	20 B2 AA	32 178 170
DarkCyan	00 8B 8B	0 139 139
Teal	00 80 80	0 128 128
Aqua	00 FF FF	0 255 255
Cyan	00 FF FF	0 255 255
LightCyan	E0 FF FF	224 255 255
PaleTurquoise	AF EE EE	175 238 238
Aquamarine	7F FF D4	127 255 212
Turquoise	40 E0 D0	64 224 208
MediumTurquoise	48 D1 CC	72 209 204
DarkTurquoise	00 CE D1	0 206 209
CadetBlue	5F 9E A0	95 158 160
SteelBlue	46 82 B4	70 130 180
LightSteelBlue	B0 C4 DE	176 196 222
PowderBlue	B0 E0 E6	176 224 230
LightBlue	AD D8 E6	173 216 230
SkyBlue	87 CE EB	135 206 235
LightSkyBlue	87 CE FA	135 206 250
DeepSkyBlue	00 BF FF	0 191 255
DodgerBlue	1E 90 FF	30 144 255
CornflowerBlue	64 95 ED	100 149 237
MediumSlateBlue	7B 68 EE	123 104 238
RoyalBlue	41 69 E1	65 105 225
Blue	00 00 FF	0 0 255

Name	Hex Code RGB	Decimal Code
MediumBlue	00 00 CD	0 0 205
DarkBlue	00 00 8B	0 0 139
Navy	00 00 80	0 0 128
MidnightBlue	19 19 70	25 25 112
Cornsilk	FF F8 DC	255 248 220
BlanchedAlmond	FF EB CD	255 235 205
Bisque	FF E4 C4	255 228 196
NavajoWhite	FF DE AD	255 222 173
Wheat	F5 DE B3	245 222 179
BurlyWood	DE B8 87	222 184 135
Tan	D2 B4 8C	210 180 140
RosyBrown	BC 8F 8F	188 143 143
SandyBrown	F4 A4 60	244 164 96
Goldenrod	DA A5 20	218 165 32
DarkGoldenrod	B8 86 0B	184 134 11
Peru	CD 85 3F	205 133 63
Chocolate	D2 69 1E	210 105 30
SaddleBrown	8B 45 13	139 69 19
Sienna	A0 52 2D	160 82 45
Brown	A5 2A 2A	165 42 42
Maroon	80 00 00	128 0 0
White	FF FF FF	255 255 255
Snow	FF FA FA	255 250 250
Honeydew	F0 FF F0	240 255 240
MintCream	F5 FF FA	245 255 250
Azure	F0 FF FF	240 255 255
AliceBlue	F0 F8 FF	240 248 255
GhostWhite	F8 F8 FF	248 248 255
WhiteSmoke	F5 F5 F5	245 245 245
Seashell	FF F5 EE	255 245 238
Beige	F5 F5 DC	245 245 220
OldLace	FD F5 E6	253 245 230
FloralWhite	FF FA F0	255 250 240
Ivory	FF FF F0	255 255 240
AntiqueWhite	FA EB D7	250 235 215
Linen	FA F0 E6	250 240 230
LavenderBlush	FF F0 F5	255 240 245
MistyRose	FF E4 E1	255 228 225
Gainsboro	DC DC DC	220 220 220
LightGrey	D3 D3 D3	211 211 211
Silver	C0 C0 C0	192 192 192
DarkGrey	A9 A9 A9	169 169 169
Grey	80 80 80	128 128 128
DimGrey	69 69 69	105 105 105
LightSlateGrey	77 88 99	119 136 153
SlateGrey	70 80 90	112 128 144
DarkSlateGrey	2F 4F 4F	47 79 79
Black	00 00 00	0 0 0

Types of colour

Previously, we looked at RGB and CMYK. The colours used in each of these colour spaces can be described with great precision in distinct ways.

Colour for print

Accurate colour reproduction in print can be ensured by using swatch books, such as the Pantone PMS system, to specify the colours used. The Pantone swatch books use the Pantone Colour Matching System, which is explained below. It is important to store the books away from direct light otherwise the colours will fade and lose their precision.

Colour for screen

Web-safe colours are a group of 216 colours that are considered to be safe for use in the design of web pages. This palette came into being when computer monitors were only able to display 256 colours and were chosen to match the colour palettes of leading web browsers of the time. The web-safe colour palette has the highest number of distinct colours within which each colour can be distinguished individually. On-screen colour can be controlled using web-safe colours to ensure consistent colour reproduction regardless of the screen a web page is being viewed on. The main web-safe colours are shown below and the full set shown opposite.

Colours are represented in HTML using a hex triplet, a six-digit, three-byte hexadecimal number. Each byte refers to either red, green or blue (in that order) with a range of 00 to FF (hexadecimal notation) or 0 to 255 (decimal notation) to represent the minimum and maximum intensity of each colour component. For example, the yellow below has a decimal value of 255, 255, 0, which in hexadecimal becomes the FFFF00 hex triplet.

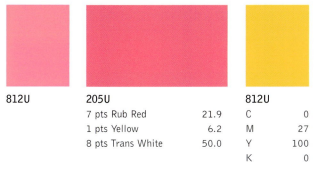

812U	205U		812U	
	7 pts Rub Red	21.9	C	0
	1 pts Yellow	6.2	M	27
	8 pts Trans White	50.0	Y	100
			K	0

Pantone PMS books

The main Pantone swatch books are Process (colours made up of CMYK) and Solid (special colours) and both come in coated and uncoated versions. There are also swatch books for metallics and pastels. The first colour chip above is special colour 812U, and the U means it is for uncoated stock (C means coated). The second chip is a solid colour made by mixing Rubine Red with yellow and white. Mixing allows a printer to make a large gamut of colours from a small set of inks. The final chip is a process colour made from percentages of the cyan, magenta, yellow and black process colours.

White	#FFFFFF	
Silver	#C0C0C0	
Grey	#808080	
Black	#000000	
Red	#FF0000	
Maroon	#800000	
Yellow	#FFFF00	
Olive	#808000	
Lime	#00FF00	
Green	#008000	
Aqua	#00FFFF	
Teal	#008080	
Blue	#0000FF	
Navy	#000080	
Fuschia	#FF00FF	
Purple	#800080	

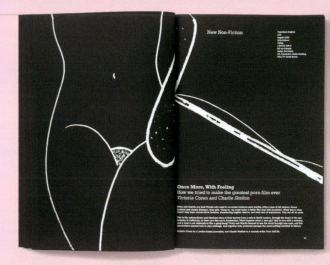

4th Estate ↑ →

In a world where four-colour printing has become established as a minimum requirement, Frost Design shows that black and white is still an effective 'colour' choice with these minimalist designs for 4th Estate. They depict items that we are used to seeing in vibrant colour, such as people's eyes or the human body. These monochrome spreads feature designs in white that are reversed out of full-bleed black flood colour.

Design: Frost Design

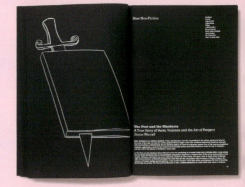

I LOVE THE REST OF MY LIFE
THOUGH IT IS TRANSITORY
LIKE A LIGHT AZURE MORNING GLORY.

Broadgate   ←   ↙

In this brochure for Broadgate
health club, a series of haiku
poems punctuate the
aspirational imagery. Colour is
used to reinforce the meaning
of the poem. Bold type is
carefully set and softened
through the use of flat, flood
colours. The spreads feature
the use of flood colour in which
the title haiku has been
reversed out of the flat colour,
creating a bold and engaging
set of statements.

Design: Studio Myerscough

specials or spot colours

On the previous spreads, we looked at how the four-colour printing process can reproduce a wide range of colours. There are, however, colours that can be printed outside of this range of colours. These colours include metallics, fluorescent colours, and a range of delicate pastel colours. These special or spot colours print as flat colours – they print on their own printing plate in the same way that cyan, magenta, yellow and black do in CMYK printing.

In essence, in four-colour printing each of the subtractive primaries CMY (cyan, magenta and yellow) print as special colours, and are combined to create a variety of other colours. The use of special colours can create great visual impact (as shown opposite), or can be used to ensure that consistent colours are used over a variety of printing jobs.

This square was printed by the four-colour printing process. If you look closely, you will see that it is made up of cyan, magenta, yellow and black dots. The four-colour process can produce nearly all colours by combining the three process colours in different ratios. Although this process can produce a wide range of colours, it also has limitations, which means that a 'special' colour may need to be used, as shown opposite.

Date of Birth   ↓
This identity uses a silver metallic ink, printed onto a matt black Colour Plan stock.

Design: Planning Unit

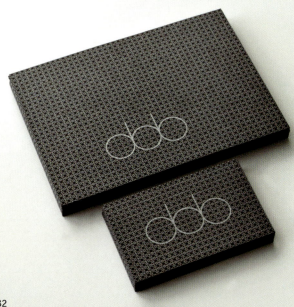

Spot colour
A spot colour is a pre-mixed ink colour usually identified by a colour system (for example, PMS) that is used for documents requiring few colours or specific colours. Spot colour is applied as a separate plate and will appear smooth when viewed closely.

Metallics
These are inks that contain metallic particles so they appear like metals such as silver, gold and copper. Metallic inks may tarnish or scuff, so applying a protective varnish may be necessary.

Fluorescent colours
These inks are so brilliant that they appear to give off light. Fluorescent inks can achieve bright colours, particularly on coloured stocks, but they need to be printed in higher concentrations than normal inks in order to achieve the intensity required.

Hexachrome
Pantone has developed a six-colour printing process called Hexachrome that enhances the CMYK system by adding orange and green. The extended colour range enriches photographic reproduction and accurate simulation of all PMS spot colours.

This page was printed using a special or spot colour. If you look closely, you will see that it is a solid colour and not made up of dots like the square on the opposite page, which was produced using the four-colour printing process. A special colour is one that cannot be made using the CMYK process colours and they include metallic, fluorescent and Pantone (PMS) inks that must be applied using additional plates. One common usage of special colours is for corporate logos. Although more expensive, the advantage is obvious – the design is printed in a precise, defined colour.

Pages 129, 136 and 137 are also printed using PMS 812

colour combinations

A design typically has a dominant colour with subordinate and accent colours. The colour palette selection will depend upon the message, mood or tone that is to be conveyed by a design. With a plethora of possible colour combinations available, the colour wheel can be used as a tool to make colour palette selections that result in harmonious combinations, as shown below. Selecting split complements, mutual complements or triads (see page 127) of the principal colour will provide a convenient short cut for selecting a palette.

Subordinate
A visually weaker colour that complements or contrasts with the dominant colour.

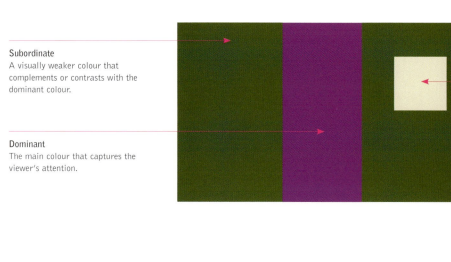

Accent
This colour is used to provide a sympathetic visual detail.

Dominant
The main colour that captures the viewer's attention.

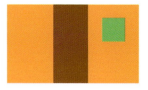   

Palette creation

Different colour combinations infuse a design with different levels of intensity, energy and feeling. They can be natural or vibrant, bold and energetic, or calm, as the examples above show. A powerful palette that uses a dark colour combined with one or two authoritative colours, such as a vibrant yellow – like the warning markings on animals and insects – makes a definite statement. Softer colours, such as pastels, create diffused colour that is subtle and delicate; they provide good contrast to a bolder primary or accent colour. The use of a rich purple adds an exotic or mysterious touch, while the use of blues will give a cool and relaxed feel to a design, adding a touch of conservatism or traditionalism.

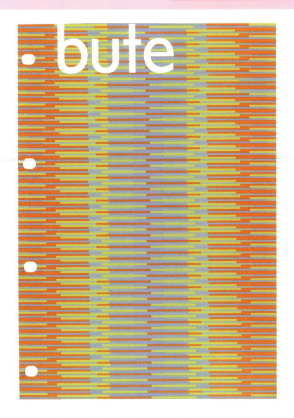

Bute ↘ ↗

This is the identity and branding for Scottish textile manufacturer Bute. Taking inspiration from the product, the literature suite uses colour as a means of navigation. The simple silk-screened folder (top left) contains an intro card (top right), a brochure featuring the product (below left), and a series of coloured gatefold fabric swatches (below right).

Design: Studio Myerscough

colouring images

A colour image is produced by separating it into the three trichromatic colours – cyan, magenta and yellow – and black, the process colours utilized in colour printing. Nearly all colours can be printed using these subtractive primaries in the four-colour printing process, using a separate printing plate for each colour to build the image as shown below. However, the designer does not have to settle for the original colours of an image. By using some of the following options, the dramatic nature of an image can be changed and enhanced considerably, as shown opposite.

Below are the CMYK colour separations needed to produce a full-colour image. Each colour film is made up of dots that, when printed over the other films in registration, produce the image (far left). The dots for each colour are aligned at different angles so that they overlap to produce the image. They are too small to see with the naked eye, but the pattern they form is shown in the enlarged image (left). The printing process prints in the order CMYK and builds the image up in this way (below).

Cyan
(C)

Cyan and Magenta
(C+M)

Cyan, Magenta and Yellow
(C+M+Y)

Cyan, Magenta, Yellow and Black
(C+M+Y+K)

Original four-colour CMYK image
This is the basic photograph.

Greyscale image
A greyscale is an image formed by the shades of grey from black through to white.

Greyscale image with the picture converted to magenta
A greyscale, when saved as a TIFF (Tagged Information File Format), can be coloured directly in desktop publishing programs.

Greyscale image with the picture converted to 50% black and the background printing as 100% yellow
The background can be coloured independently from the image.

Duotone image with equal parts of black and cyan

Duotone image of black and 100% cyan

Duotone image with equal parts of cyan and yellow

Duotone image with equal parts of magenta and cyan with opposite values

Tritone image with equal parts of black, red and orange

Quadtone image with equal parts of black, red, orange and yellow

Bitmap image with 50% threshold
A bitmap is formed by a pattern of pixels and records information as blacks and whites only.

Coloured bitmap
Bitmaps can be coloured in the same way as greyscale images – here it is coloured as a fluorescent.

137

Additional techniques

Colour can be used in many different ways to add an element of creativity to a design and present images in a non-standard way. The techniques below dramatically change the presentation of an image, which leads the viewer to read or interpret them differently.

Duotone gradient
A colour gradient that creates a duotone can add subtle texture and interest to an image.

Effects
There are many effects for adjusting images; for example, a sepia tint can make an image appear like a vintage photograph.

Tint
The specific percentage value of a colour from 0 to 100%. Very low values may not reproduce in the printing process.

Overprint
An overprint is where one ink prints over another ink. This can result in the creation of another colour or the production of a deeper black.

Reverse out
Where a design is produced by being removed from a block of printed colour and left as an unprinted area.

Surprint
A printing technique that uses tint values of a single colour to give the impression that two or more colours are used.

Flood colour

Flood colour is the practice of filling a volume of space with highly saturated colour. In design, an entire page or space may be filled, or flooded, with one colour that bleeds off the page.

colour as branding

So far we have looked at how colour can be used, the technical aspects of its use and what it means. Colour does not work in isolation, but in conjunction with typography, illustration, format and layout to create a design. In branding, colour contributes a very specific facet – instant recognition.

Difference and similarity

Some product groups tend to use similar colour language to convey the same values to the consumer. In the supermarket, we see clusters of dark or mint green in the frozen vegetable section, which could represent freshness, while gold is widely used to represent quality or exclusivity. An identity is often created through the use of a single colour across the product range of a brand. While reinforcing the visual identity of a brand, this can also run the risk of becoming visually stale. This can be avoided by allowing each product that is part of a brand to have certain unique elements in the way colour or images are used.

Colour consistency

Companies expend a great deal of effort defining their brands and brand image. As colour plays an important part in this, it is paramount that the application of colour values is consistent. Often, the colours used will be precisely expressed in PMS spot colours with usage guidelines to maintain consistent usage across design agencies, printers, suppliers and others that need to work with the brand.

breathe the fresh air of novelty and take pleasure in the details, in your renewed everyday scenery. if this is life, it is created for you. enjoy!

if & for ↙ → ↓

This identity for Greek concept goods shop uses typography and colour creatively to attention-grabbing effect. The language used is simple, direct and sparse, as the messaging and typography are stripped to their basic elements, dispensing with majuscules and punctuation. The use of cyan creates a visual break in the copy and adds a hierarchy or structure in place of the absent capitals and full stops, which helps create a strong and memorable identity. A simple, honest and utilitarian approach to design.

Design: The Design Shop

Emotional swings / Colour combinations

Exercise #1 – Emotional swings

Premise
Colour usage surrounds us in printed and digital media due to its power to communicate and add dynamism and emotion to a design.

Exercise
Select an image or photograph and give it different colour treatments to see how each one changes the message the image or design communicates.

Outcome
Produce a visualization of your findings showing how different colour treatments create different emotions or readings of the design or image. For example, you may present results that are upbeat, happy, sad, traditional or futuristic.

Aim
To encourage a more considered appreciation of colour use in design.

Colour treatments ↑ ↙

A colour image captures a moment in time. Colour details in the image convey information that help us construct meaning. Changing the colour detail enables a designer to present different meanings and emotions.

stand out

blend in

clash

Juxtaposition ↓ ←

Certain colour combinations create a visual effect that fools or misleads the eye. Although all the rectangles below are the same size, some will appear nearer than others. Equally, being able to control colours allows a designer to make items stand out, blend in, or even intentionally clash.

Exercise #2 – Colour combinations

Premise
Colours are affected by other colours around them. A light colour tends to close in when it surrounds a dark colour, and expand out when it is positioned within a dark colour.

Exercise
Create a series of typographic statements that exploit the above illusions in how we see colours.

Outcome
A series of large-scale posters.

Aim
To think about how colours affect meaning.

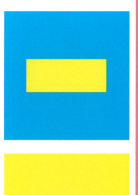

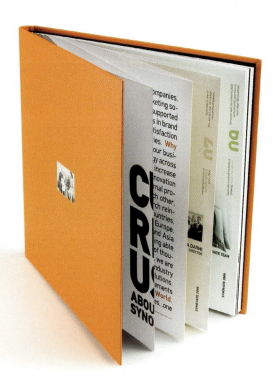

Print finishing

Print finishing covers all the aspects of how a final design is brought to the realization of the final product. This includes elements such as what printing inks and printing techniques are used, the stock(s) that a job is printed on, as well as the use of different finishing techniques, such as die-cutting, folding, embossing and binding.

While print finishing techniques increase the cost of a print job, their careful application adds dynamism to a piece. A clear understanding of print finishing techniques and their potential impact will enable you to use them cost-effectively. Even within tighter budgets, print finishing methods can facilitate a high level of creativity without breaking the bank.

Synovate ←

This is a corporate brochure produced for Synovate, a global market research company. Each brochure was designed to have a unique cover with bold typography to communicate the company's standards for excellence and a dynamic culture.

Design: Mouse Graphics

paper types

Having a sound knowledge of paper types will be crucial when making decisions on the appropriateness of a particular stock. Some stocks are selected for their physical look and feel; others are used for how they reproduce texts and/or images. It is also worth considering how certain stocks 'behave'. Certain papers have additional 'quirks' (for example, 'showthrough' as shown below). This spread provides a guide to some of the main paper types and their inherent qualities.

Weight

The weight of paper is part of its specification and is measured in grammes per square metre (GSM). It is based on the weight of a square metre of the stock. The higher the GSM value, the heavier and stiffer a stock is.

Thickness

Also known as 'caliper' or 'bulk', thickness refers to how deep a sheet of paper is. Thicker stocks tend to be stiffer and more opaque. Thinner stocks can have more showthrough.

Deckle edge

This is the ragged edge of the paper as it leaves the papermaking machine. Machine-made paper has two deckle edges, while handmade paper has four. Typically cut away, a deckle edge can add a decorative effect when left. The effect can be imitated by tearing the edge of the paper by hand. This is also known as 'feather edge'.

Wove

This a type of paper that shows few differences in texture and thickness when held to light. Wove paper is produced by pressing the pulp against a very fine mesh to produce a virtually uniform texture that is not ribbed or watermarked.

Showthrough

A quality that allows what is printed on one side of a sheet to show through and be visible on the other. Showthrough is caused by inadequate paper opacity. High opacity papers have no show through. This is not to be confused with 'strike-through', where the liquid element of a printing ink penetrates through the sheet.

Finish

The surface characteristics of the paper, including its feel and appearance. From matt and dull to smooth and glossy, paper finishes can be applied offline or during the production process.

Opacity

The extent to which a stock does not allow the transmission of light. High opacity papers do not show through what is printed on the other side of the sheet. Low opacity papers allow showthrough.

Grain

The alignment of fibres during the paper manufacturing process in the direction that the sheet passes through the papermaking machine. The grain is the direction that most of the fibres lay. This characteristic means that paper is easier to fold, bend or tear along its grain direction.

Handmade paper with unaligned fibres

Bible paper with low bulk and high opacity

Coated paper that holds a good colour image

Coated

Paper made with a mineral, starch or polymer layer spread over the surface during manufacturing to improve its characteristics and printability. Coating minerals such as kaolin clay, calcium carbonate and talc improve whiteness, brightness and surface printability.

Uncoated

Paper produced without a coating layer to enhance printability. May use mineral fillers to improve whiteness. It is the largest printing and writing paper category and includes almost all office photocopy paper, stationery and offset grades used for general commercial printing.

Newsprint

A paper stock made primarily of mechanically ground wood pulp. Newsprint is a cheap stock used for high volume printing, but it has a shorter lifespan than other grades. Its low quality, rough surface and comparatively high absorbency means image reproduction capacity is mediocre compared to other stocks.

Matt

An uncoated stock used for inkjet printing that produces quality prints, but without vibrant colour finish. Matt paper produces non-glare images that are not vulnerable to being marred by fingerprints.

Chromolux

A heavyweight, high caliper and high quality cast-coated paper with an extremely smooth and high-gloss surface. It has a waterproof coating on a single side.

Handmade paper

Paper made individually by hand using cotton, silk or other materials in a mould and deckle. The mould is a frame covered with a flat screen, which is covered by a flat deckle or frame that contains the wet pulp run-off. Handmade paper fibres do not have a grain.

Bible or India paper

A thin, lightweight, long-life, opaque paper typically made from 25% cotton and linen rags or flax with chemical wood pulp named after its most common usage. Bible paper allows a higher number of pages within a given spine size due to its low caliper.

Flock

Paper coated with a fine woollen refuse or vegetable fibre dust that is fixed with glue to provide a velvety or cloth-like appearance. Flock adds a tactile and alternative visual element and, while it does not provide a good printing surface, it can be used to good effect with foil-blocking.

Radical Architecture ↑ ↙

The strong constructivist colour scheme and manifesto-style catalogue combine to create an impactful exhibition. The catalogue, printed on wafer-thin Bible stock, is printed as a series of individual pads, allowing visitors to take selected pages. The typography is intentionally small with long line lengths, necessitating visitors to retain the manifesto sections for later reading. The showthrough of the stock, (shown above) becomes part of the design.

Design: Studio Myerscough

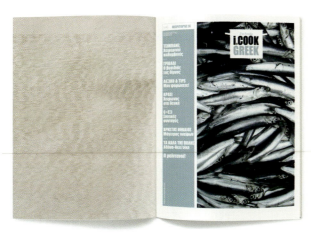

I Cook Greek   ↑   ↓

The manifesto style text statements add drama and character to these designs promoting Greek food.

Design: Mouse Graphics

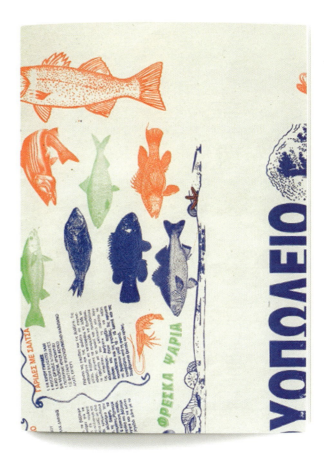

paper engineering

Paper engineering here refers to the construction of three-dimensional shapes and structures from paper, often by folding, rather than the manufacture of the paper itself. Paper can be used to produce geometric objects such as cubes, plants and animals. These are also seen in origami and the interactive pages in pop-up books.

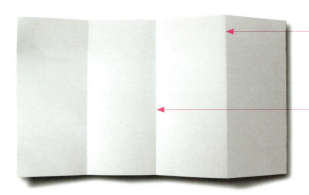

Mountain fold

Held horizontally, a mountain fold has a central crease at the top, like a mountain ridge, with the panels falling downwards.

Valley fold

Held horizontally, a valley fold has a central crease at the bottom with the panels rising upwards to form the valley sides.

Daniel Libeskind mailer ↑

A fundraising mailer for Daniel Libeskind's proposed extension to the V&A takes on a three-dimensional structure. The outer packaging collapses to reveal a model of the complicated 24-plane continuous spiral construction: 'If the best way to understand the building was to look at a model, hey, let's send people a model,' explains Johnson Banks.

Design: Johnson Banks

Fena – Depth of Style   ↑   →

This brochure for Greek clothing store, Fena, uses a composition of printed items and paper engineering to create different layers and shadows (above) that are then photographed (top) to produce the final composite design (right). The final production appears to be three dimensional due to the shadow effects captured in the photographs.

Design: Beetroot

lithography and CTP

Lithography is a printing process that uses a smooth printing plate that functions on the basis that oil and water repel each other. The image is applied to the plate as a polymer that repels water, but accepts ink. When the plate passes under the ink roller, non-image areas that have a water film repel the oily inks that stick to the image areas. Lithography produces good photographic reproduction and fine linework on a variety of stocks. Printing plates are easy to prepare and high speeds are achievable, making it a low-cost printing method, whether on sheet-fed or continuous web presses.

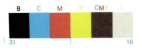

On the left is a series of repeating predefined colours printed along the edge of a sheet that are used by press operators to check that a press is printing consistently.

Cyan

Cyan and Magenta

Cyan, Magenta and Yellow

Cyan, Magenta, Yellow and Black

Four-colour print process

This uses four subtractive primary process colour inks to reproduce colour images. Cyan, magenta and yellow are subtractive primaries that are combined via printing to make the additive primaries (red, green and blue) of visible light. Different colours are created by mixing the process colours in different concentrations. Black is added separately as the black produced by mixing the three subtractive primaries is unsatisfactory.

Computer-to-plate

An imaging technology used in printing whereby a design is output directly onto a printing plate. Traditional printing methods see a design output onto film that is then used to make a printing plate.

Computer-to-plate technology thus results in a quicker and cheaper method for making printing plates, while a sharper and more detailed image is transferred, with reduced risk of registration problems.

Web printing

A high-volume printing method where printing presses are fed by a continuous roll of paper providing greater economies of scale than sheet-fed printing. Once printed, the pages are separated and cut to size.

Sheet-fed printing

A medium-volume printing method where printing presses are fed by individual sheets that may be folded and cut to size once printed.

Contrast   ↑   →

This poster for a video projection project, organized by the Greek
Graphic Design Association during the European Design Awards,
features the use of a very clear grid to place the different pieces
of information that brings order and structure to the content.
Each poster was printed with different contrasts, or tint value (as
can be seen above), to reflect the theme of the exhibition.

Design: The Design Shop

four-colour tints

The reproduction of colour is created by screening the three trichromatic process colours cyan, magenta and yellow – usually in 10% increments – that when combined with one or both of the other colours form all the permutations shown opposite. There are 1,000 tints available using the three process colours and a further 300 colours obtainable by combining a single process colour with black. The three charts shown at the top of the opposite page demonstrate the 100 colour variations available by using a single process colour in combination with black. The remaining 11 charts are mixes of magenta and cyan in combination with varying increments of yellow.

The tint diagrams on the opposite page are designed to provide a clear visual indication of the true representation obtained by using four-colour tints.

It is important to be aware that these representations are only as accurate as the standard four-colour printing process and its limitations. The stock that this page is printed on will also affect the reproduction of the colour combinations, as will any stock you use.

The black and yellow chart below demonstrates how to determine the values of a chosen colour. The top left-hand corner of the chart is 0% yellow with 0% black, hence nothing prints. The chart gives the range of colours at 10% increments of both yellow and black through to 100% yellow and 100% black in the bottom right-hand corner, which prints as a solid colour.

By drawing a line vertically and horizontally from a selected colour, one can establish its component parts. In the example below, the selected colour is produced using 40% black and 60% yellow.

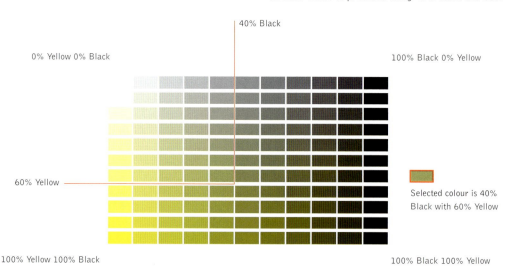

40% Black

0% Yellow 0% Black

100% Black 0% Yellow

60% Yellow

Selected colour is 40% Black with 60% Yellow

100% Yellow 100% Black

100% Black 100% Yellow

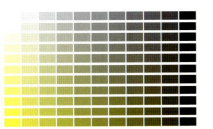

Four colour tints of black and yellow

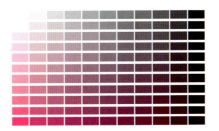

Four colour tints of black and magenta

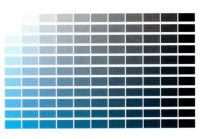

Four colour tints of black and cyan

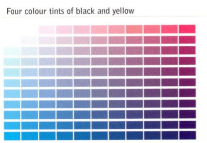

Four colour tints of magenta and cyan with 0% yellow

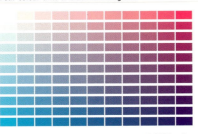

Four colour tints of magenta and cyan with 10% yellow

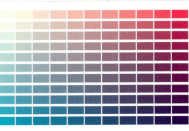

Four colour tints of magenta and cyan with 20% yellow

Four colour tints of magenta and cyan with 30% yellow

Four colour tints of magenta and cyan with 40% yellow

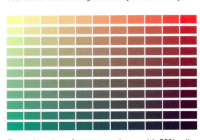

Four colour tints of magenta and cyan with 50% yellow

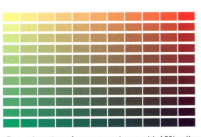

Four colour tints of magenta and cyan with 60% yellow

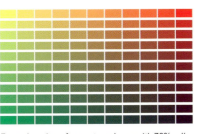

Four colour tints of magenta and cyan with 70% yellow

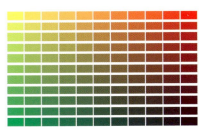

Four colour tints of magenta and cyan with 80% yellow

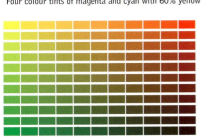

Four colour tints of magenta and cyan with 90% yellow

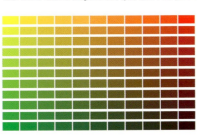

Four colour tints of magenta and cyan with 100% yellow

Additional techniques

Various techniques can be used to adjust and correct the output of a printing press in order to produce different printed effects, such as ink trapping and overprinting.

Ink trapping

Ink trapping is the adjustment of areas of coloured text or shapes to account for misregistration on the printing press by overlapping them slightly. This is required as the halftone dots that make up printed images overlap because they are of different sizes and at different screen angles. The colours are overlapped to prevent the appearance of white gaps where they are supposed to meet. This process, however, is not necessary for photographic images.

Ink trapping also prevents undesired colours being formed when colours unintentionally overlap. Trapping is affected by how dry the original ink layer is and the ink film thickness of subsequent layers

printed over it. The trap is normally created with the lighter colour, and it is either spread (enlarged) or choked (reduced) into darker colours to combine them in the area where they join.

Trapping is important on black text because the fineness (usually) of text means it is hard to register with surrounding colours. When trapped properly, the black is overprinted on the surrounding area. Trapping is used on black and very dark colours as the change in colour is barely noticeable.

All items knockout

All items overprint

Overprinting

This occurs when ink overprints on another in the printing process to create a different colour. Overprinting can produce creative effects and extend colour options when printing with a limited range of inks, such as two colours. The illustrations above show colours printing without overprinting (above left) and overprinting (above right). Notice how the colours create new colours when they overprint.

According to colour theory, overprinting pairs of the three subtractive primary CMY process colours produce additive primary colours. To overprint effectively, a designer needs to bear in mind the order that the process colours print in. If printing in the order cyan, magenta, yellow and black, the yellow obviously cannot overprint cyan for example. Blacks with different tones and intensities can also be achieved by overprinting.

Bouncers and shiners

When is black not black? Black is a colour that is not always what it seems when reproduced by the four-colour printing process. While it may do a great job of creating good shadow tone in full-colour images, when left on its own it looks pale and washed out. Where there are large areas of black to be printed in four colours, it is often advisable to use a cyan shiner. A shiner is typically a 50% or 60%

cyan area behind the black that helps to improve the visual density and saturation. Cyan is the best of the other three process colours to use as a shiner as yellow and magenta result in a muddy black or one that looks artificially warm.

Black has a large part to play in the problem of bouncers. Bounce is a registration problem that can be avoided with the use of a 100% black that also contains amounts of cyan, magenta and yellow. A four-colour black results in a

much fuller and richer black as shown above, and having at least one shared colour between adjacent objects makes errors in registration less noticeable.

A Fusion in Print
Through our expertise
in print and pre-press
services, we work
with designers to
create effective and
challenging print.

To find out more
about Team, contact
Simon Bucktrout
on 0790 049 3690
or email simon@
team-impression.com

Team Impression
Fusion House
1 Lockwood Close
Leeds LS11 5UU

0113 272 4800 Ph
0113 272 4801 Fx
0113 272 4807 iSDN

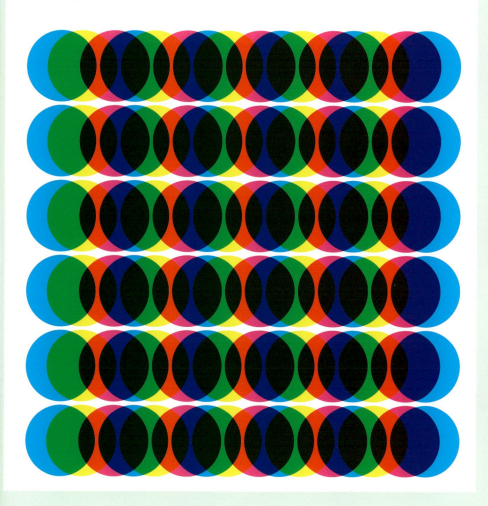

Team ←

This poster for Leeds-based
printers, Team Impression,
uses an overprint of Cyan,
Magenta and Yellow super-
sized dots. The dot motif is a
representation of the four-
colour printing process.

Design: Design Project

157

fore-edge printing

When considering printing, we tend to think of ink being applied to the front face of a sheet of paper. Fore-edge printing rethinks this by printing to the side of a book. This creative process maximizes impact by utilizing space that is not normally considered or valued. Another quirk of this type of printing is that it alters as the user bends and fans the book. There are two ways of achieving this effect. Firstly, by printing the main text pages, binding and then printing the text block directly. Alternatively, you can print bleeding off the outside edge of the page, and this will give an effect of the fore-edge being printed. This book for example, uses a colour block in the top right hand corner, acting as an index device.

Made You Look ↓

New York design studio Sagmeister Inc chose to use fore-edge printing in this volume of work entitled Made You Look. The book has two images printed along the fore-edge that are only revealed when the book is flexed. Flexed one way the book's title is revealed. Flexed the other way, the dog gets something to eat.

Design: Sagmeister Inc

American Photography 15 → ↓

Sagmeister Inc used a similar concept in its design for a book about American photography for Amilus Inc. The only recognizable image on the outside surfaces of the book is the landscape revealed by flexing the pages. The curious image on the cover (far right) takes image manipulation to one extreme. It contains compressed versions of all the photographs in the book.

Design: Sagmeister Inc

screen-printing

Screen-printing is a low-volume printing method that sees a viscous ink passed through a screen that holds a design onto a substrate. A screen made from silk or synthetic fibres supports a stencil carrying an image to print on virtually any surface. The viscous inks used provide a tactile element to a design. Screen-printing is not restricted to the four process colours of offset lithography and can apply special colours to a design, including white ink. Screen-print quality is affected by two factors: mesh count and mesh grade. Mesh count refers to the number of threads per inch of the screen. The lower the count, the less support there is for detail and the heavier the deposit of ink. Mesh grade refers to the thread thickness, which influences the weight of the ink film. There are four grades: S, M, T and HD. S is the thinnest giving 50%–70% open area, and HD the heaviest giving 20%–35% open area.

The basic equipment for screen-printing: viscous inks, a spatula and a squeegee that sit upon a screen that is supported by a sturdy wooden frame.

A design is cut out and attached to the screen so that ink will pass through the screen and the image areas of the design. Ink is applied to the screen with a spatula and spread along its width. The squeegee is pulled from the top of the frame, holding the screen to the bottom with continuous and even weight to push the ink through the screen and design onto the substrate.

Haçienda ↑ →

This poster features an intriguing array of typeface styles over an amorphous yellow shape that was screen-printed for the seventh anniversary of Manchester's legendary Haçienda nightclub. The Haçienda brand was so well-known that little information needed to be given other than the date. The brand itself, reduced to its highly identifiable first three letters 'Haç' stretches across the poster over Fac 51, an equally familiar brand mark of the club. Several special inks, including a luminescent, are used to create a poster that functions effectively in the early hours – when the intended audience is most likely to see it!

Design: 8vo

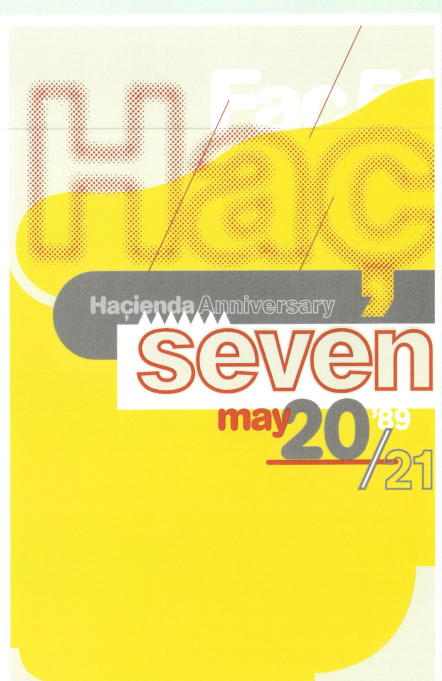

letterpress

Letterpress is a method of relief printing whereby an inked, raised surface is pressed against the paper. It was the first ever commercial printing method and is the source of many printing terms. The raised surface that makes the impression is typically made from pieces of type, but photo-engraved plates can also be used. Letterpress printing can be identified by the sharp and precise edges to letters and their heavier ink border.

A defect of letterpress is appealing to modern designers. When improperly inked, patches appear in the letters giving them a uniqueness where each impression is subtly different. This can be seen in the cards below, printed by Forme London, for the Royal Academy of Arts.

Royal Academy of Arts ↓

This defect can be used to evoke nostalgia for a bygone era. The circus-inspired bill posters for the Royal Academy of Arts designed by Abbott Mead Vickers BBDO were set and printed by Forme London using an eclectic mixture of original woodcut fonts.

Design: Abbott Mead Vickers BBDO

RSA ← ↙

The layout for the Royal Society of Arts (RSA) annual report is deliberately kept simple and easily accessible for its target audience. It was important that the report did not look too corporate, nor give the impression that the organization was in need of sponsorship. The result is short, uncluttered and discursive. The use of distinct letterpress typography, often used as illustration, adds a layering of information and a textural quality.

Design: Atelier Works

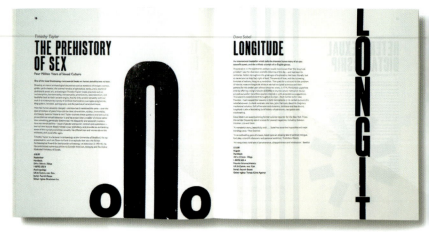

4th Estate ↑ ↗

The dramatic example of mixing type sizes and letterpress printing can be seen in this catalogue for 4th Estate. It uses a sans-serif font set in majuscules or uppercase – the sheer scale and clean lines of the characters serve to divide and organize the page. The type is used as an organizational device, while also performing a textural role. In the image below, it is possible to read the text but requires some effort as words are set in conflicting directions. This is a deliberately produced paradox because it is a contents page.

Design: Frost Design

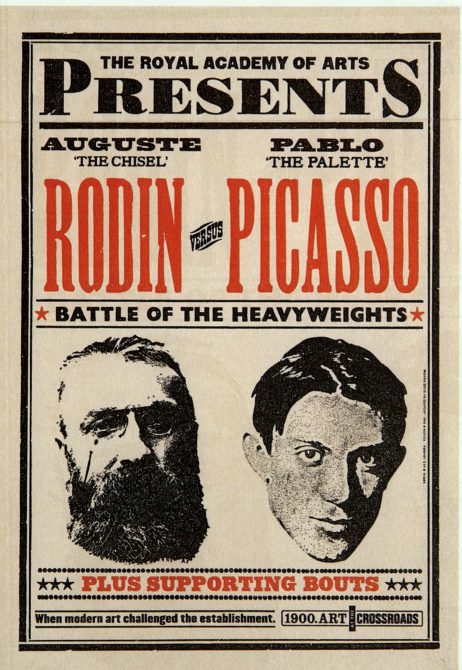

The Royal Academy of Arts
←

This invitation demonstrates the beauty of letterpress forms. The type, set in the style of an eighteenth-century boxing poster, was sourced from a large collection of woodblock forms.

Design: Abbott Mead Vickers • BBDO, printing by Forme London

hot metal type

Hot metal, also known as hot type composition or cast metal, refers to the process of casting the type in lines in molten metal. Text is typed into a machine to produce a punched paper tape that controls the characters cast by the casting machine. Hot metal type made it possible to create large quantities of type in a relatively inexpensive fashion.

Moveable type

Moveable type was the next leap from the earliest printing presses that used a wooden block carved with the text. This sped up the production of individual pages, but meant a new block had to be carved for each page. Moveable type is a typesetting method that uses single pieces of type that can be set in a block and printed. Each character is moveable and can be used again.

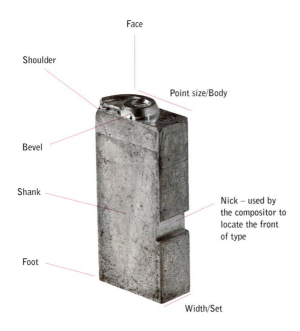

Face

Shoulder

Point size/Body

Bevel

Shank

Nick – used by the compositor to locate the front of type

Foot

Width/Set

Alexander McQueen ↑

Alexander McQueen was inspired by Stanley Kubrick's film, The Shining, for a fashion show and created an invite to match. This was printed by letterpress in order to impart a heavy indent into the substrate to give the impression that each invite was individually typed on a typewriter. The invite mimics the 'All work and no play makes Jack a dull boy' scene from Kubrick's film.

Design: Studio Myerscough, printing by Forme London

And now for something completely different...

Funny thing, comedy. As soft as Charlie Chaplin fluttering his love-lorn lashes, as brutal as the Three Stooges poking each other's eyes out. As daft as Mr Bean, as deft as Groucho Marx's verbal napalming of the monumentally fireproof Margaret Dumont. A curious art indeed, to amplify and project images of our weakness and wonderfulness and have us love it. We laugh; and as Herman Melville's Billy Budd said, laughter is good.

Morgan Stanley Dean Witter ↑ ↓

These direct mail pieces use pure, understated typography, combining a sans serif header and a more characterful body copy that is all set in hot metal type. This produces a deep indentation into the paper stock.

Design: E-Fact, printing by Forme London

Peace, love and understanding

For France it was Joan of Arc, for Latin America Simon Bolivar, for Cuba... well, you know. But in India, it was a frail, wire-spectacled law graduate of University College, London. Not at all your standard hero-liberator; yet somehow the fate of the entire Indian subcontinent became synonymous with one gentle, iron-willed man and his one great idea -- ahimsa, or non-violence.

The greatest

As popular icons come, he created a category all of his own – not only the supreme artist in the history of his chosen sport but also a spokesman for the underprivileged and downtrodden of America and the world. His great idea was not just to float like a butterfly and sting like a bee; it was to stand tall, believe in himself and punch above his weight. In every sense.

varnishes

A varnish is a colourless coating that is applied to a printed piece to protect the substrate from wear or smudging. Applied as a spot varnish, it also acts to enhance the visual appearance of the design or elements within it. Various varnishes are available that produce gloss, satin and matt finishes. While not strictly a varnish, UV coating can also be used to add a decorative touch to a printed piece.

Spot varnish

Spot varnish is a liquid varnish that serves as a protective coating to a printed substrate while enhancing its appearance. It can be applied to the whole page or to specific parts of it via a separate printing plate (see pages 161, 164, 165, 168, 169, 172, 173, 176).

Gloss

A gloss varnish reflects back light and is frequently used to enhance the appearance of photographs or other graphic elements in brochures, as it adds to the sharpness and saturation of images.

Matt

This varnish is typically used with text-heavy pages to diffuse light, reduce glare and so increase readability. It gives a non-glossy, smooth finish to the printed page.

Satin (or silk)

A middle option between the gloss and matt varnishes. It provides some highlight, but is not as flat as a matt finish.

Neutral

The application of a basic, almost invisible, coating that seals the printing ink without affecting the appearance of the job. It is often used to accelerate the drying of fast turnaround print jobs (such as leaflets) on matt and satin papers upon which inks dry more slowly.

UV varnish

A clear liquid that is applied like ink and cured instantly with ultraviolet light. It can provide either a gloss or matt coating. Increasingly, UV varnish is used as a spot covering to highlight a particular image because it provides more shine than varnish.

Full-bleed UV

The most common type of all-over UV coating that produces a high-gloss effect.

Textured spot UV

Textures can be created with spot UV varnish to provide an additional tactile quality to a printed piece.

Pearlescent

A varnish that subtly reflects myriad colours to give a luxurious effect.

Four-colour photograph

Four-colour photograph with spot varnish

Monochrome image

Monochrome image with 60% shiner and spot varnish

Varnish does not have to be applied across the whole image. Frequently, it is applied to highlight specific areas of a design. Notice how the discreet application of varnish can help an element jump out, such as the letter below.

Monochrome image

Monochrome image with spot varnish

physical finishing

Designers can use various print finishing techniques to change the appearance and form of a substrate without actually printing on it. These processes change the physical form of the substrate in different ways to create different visual effects and textures.

Embossing
A design that is stamped into a substrate to produce a decorative raised or indented surface using a metal die holding an image. A deboss leaves an indentation. Thinner caliper stocks hold finer lines but may tear; thicker caliper stocks are more robust but may lose fine detail. Embossed designs are usually slightly oversized, with heavier lines and extra space used than if they were going to be printed.

Duplexing
Duplexing is the bonding of two stocks to form a single substrate with different colours or textures on each side.

Perforation
Perforation or 'perf cutting' is a process that creates a cut out area in a substrate that weakens it so that it can be detached; it can also be used to create a decorative effect.

Thermography
A print finishing process that produces raised lettering by fusing thermographic powder to a design. Thermography gives a bubbly mottled surface that is highly visible, tactile and reflective.

Die cutting
A print finishing process that cuts away part of a substrate using a steel die. A die cut is mainly used for decorative purposes to enhance the visual impact of a design through the creation of interesting shapes.

Foil stamp
A print finishing process whereby a coloured foil is pressed onto a substrate via a heated die. Also called 'foil stamp', 'heat stamp' or 'foil emboss', the process allows a designer to add a shiny finish to specific design elements, such as title text. Various colours are available including metallics.

Fedrigoni ← →

This is a promotional desk calendar for a supplier of Italian printing papers. The calendar is printed on a range of coloured boards, from 250–800 micron. The outer cover features a gloss black foil on an uncoated black stock.

Design: Design Project

folding, throwouts and gatefolds

Different folding methods can be used to produce different structures for the final folded piece, which make use of the basic valley and mountain fold that sees alternate folds made in opposing directions to create a series of peaks and troughs. Each folding method requires a different imposition plan so that the pages are printed in an order that allows them to be sequential once the sheet is folded.

Keith Haring ←   ↓

This poster features the characteristic valleys and mountains of the accordion or concertina fold. Notice how this creates panels that can be used to position and organize the presentation of the text (left).

Design: Frost Design

Tammy Donohoe ↑   ↘

This catalogue features a throwup, which is similar to a throwout (see page 175) except the extra pages extend vertically rather than horizontally from the publication. The throwups allow the presentation of large-scale portrait orientation images that distinguish the publication from conventional clothing brochures.

Design: Dorian Design

virtue

ngs May 21-July 1 1997

John Virtue ←

The 16-page concertina-fold exhibition catalogue for John Virtue was produced with paintings treated in proportion. This creative use of format allows the reader to construct a miniature pop-up gallery.

Design: Studio AS

174

Throwouts and gatefolds

Throwouts and gatefolds are methods of inserting extra and/or oversize pages into a publication, typically to provide extra space to showcase a particular image or visual element.

Throwouts

A throwout is half a gatefold – it is a folded sheet bound into a publication that opens out to one side only. In opening a throwout, the extra panel is extended horizontally.

Throwup

A throwup is a folded sheet bound into a publication that opens vertically, either above or below the publication.

Gatefolds

A folded sheet showing four panels that is bound into a publication so that the right and left panels fold into the spine with parallel folds. They are used in magazines to provide extra space and are particularly useful for displaying panoramic vista images. The central panels have the same dimensions as the pages of the publication, while the outer panels are slightly narrower to allow them to nest well when folded. Gatefolds are usually numbered with letters from the page they start from, for example 32a, 32b, 32c and 32d, or they can be numbered sequentially with the pages.

Paper size
Pages of gatefolds, fold outs and the last page of accordion folds are often cut short so that they fold in and nest towards the spine of the publication.

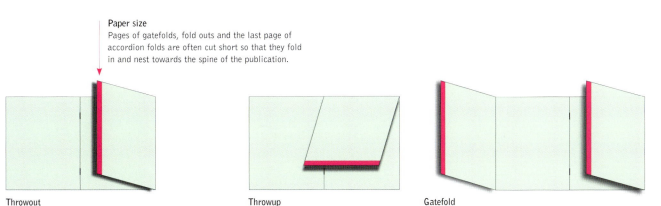

Throwout   Throwup   Gatefold

Elisabeth Frink   ↑

This catalogue uses gatefolds to provide extra space to highlight works of art – here, the dual fold out features Elisabeth Frink's sculptures.

Design: Studio AS

binding

Binding is a print finishing process that ensures the pages comprising a job are gathered and securely held together so that they function as a publication. Various types of binding are available and have different durability, aesthetic, cost and functional characteristics. Binding methods may allow pages to lay flat or not.

Perfect binding
The backs of sections are removed and held together with a flexible adhesive, which also attaches a paper cover to the spine, and the fore-edge is trimmed flat. Commonly used for paperback books.

Saddle stitch
Signatures are nested and bound with wire stitches applied through the spine along the centrefold.

Self binds
Certain publications can appear to be bound, when in fact the only print finishing process that has been used is folding. These are called self binds as the reader manually rebinds the publication after use by folding it again (maps and brochures).

Singer stitch
A thread binding in which the cover is sewn onto the book block with the stitches exposed on the cover. Singer stitch can add a decorative touch to a publication as thread is available in many weights and colours, and can be sewn in a variety of patterns.

Case or edition binding
A common hardback bookbinding method that sews signatures together, flattens the spine, and applies endsheets and head and tail bands to the spine. Hard covers are attached, the spine is usually rounded, and grooves along the cover edge act as hinges.

Canadian
A wiro-bound publication with a wraparound cover and an enclosed spine. A complete wraparound cover is a full Canadian and a partial wraparound is a half Canadian.

Open bind
An open bind sees signatures sewn together as per edition binding, but the book block is left uncovered so that the stitching remains exposed.

Z-binds
A publication produced in two sections, which are bound together by a three-panel cover that separates it into two parts. Each part shares the middle cover panel.

Pedro García →
Barcelona-based Clase designed the catalogue for Pedro García's footwear collection. A thick greyboard cover is robust enough to accept the simple heavy deboss. The immediacy of the swatch-like package is enclosed using a simple bolt fixture, implying that the contents are both bespoke and recent.
Design: Clase

Hartovasilion Bookstore ←

These are a series of sous-plats (or disposable table mats) that are perfect bound along the top edge. These single-use table mats contain 60 different designs per 'book'. This form of binding offers a simple and effective solution to the problem of fast turnaround restaurants. The energetic design also appeals to the diners' sense of humour and offers a talking point at the table.

Design: Mouse Graphics

Printed ephemera / Woodblock composition

Exercise #1 – Printed ephemera

Premise
We are surrounded by printed ephemera. We handle, use and interact with printed items on a daily basis, and are generally ignorant of how they were printed or made. Most designers, over time, develop a collection of items – a library of ephemera that they use as a reference.

Exercise
Using a loupe, collect and examine as broad a set of printed items as you can find. This could include, amongst other items, direct mail, invites, books, stamps and packaging.

Outcome
Produce a visualization of your findings. For example, you may present a breakdown of the printing and finishing methods used in the items you have collected.

Aim
To encourage a more considered appreciation of the printed items in daily life.

Loupe ←

A printer's loupe is used for looking at printed items in detail. The loupe acts like a magnifying glass, allowing us to see how an item was printed.

Woodblock letterforms can be purchased cheaply and offer an easy way to create interesting typographic forms.

Exercise #2 – Woodblock composition

Premise
We have become accustomed to adjusting point size, colour, font and other aspects of design on a computer so that design looks as we want it to look. The ability to easily alter typography causes us to forget that there is an extensive history of letterform development and printing techniques to draw inspiration from.

Exercise
Woodblock or rubber letter printing sets can be bought cheaply. Using such a set, design and print a flyer for an event, such as a party invitation. Vary the amount of ink, pressure and frequency of re-inking used.

Outcome
Without changing the design, produce several copies of the flyer – each with a different look and feel obtained solely on the basis of the printing process.

Aim
To see how varying aspects, such as ink quantity, pressure and inking frequency, affect the final design output and change its visual impact.

glossary

Accordion fold
Two or more parallel folds that open like an accordion.

Additive primaries
The red, green and blue components that together make white light.

Ascender
Part of a lower-case letter that extends above the x-height of a typeface.

Baseline
Imaginary line which the bases of all capital letters and most lower-case letters are positioned.

Baseline grid
The graphic foundation on which a design is constructed.

Bitmap
An image composed of dots.

Black printer
The film printing black in the colour separation process.

Bleed
A printed image that extends over the trim edge of the stock.

Body copy
Text that forms the main part of a work.

Body text
The matter that forms the main text of a printed book.

Bold or boldface type
A thick, heavy variety of type used to give emphasis.

Bouncers/shiners
A 50% or 60% cyan area behind the black that improves visual density and saturation.

Bowl
The curved portion of a type character.

Character
An individual element of type.

Chroma
Purity or intensity of colour.

CMYK
Cyan, magenta, yellow and black, the subtractive primaries and four process colours.

Colour separation
Photographic filtration process to divide the colours of a continuous tone-coloured original into constituent colours.

Concertina fold
Paper folding method where each fold runs opposite of the previous one to obtain a pleated outcome.

Condensed type
Type that is elongated and narrow.

Continuous tone
Continuous shades in an image, such as a photograph, that are not broken up into dots.

Contrast
The level of tone separation from white to black.

Cool colour
Green, blue and other colours with a green or blue cast.

Cropping
Trimming unwanted parts of a photograph or illustration.

Cyan
A shade of blue, one of the subtractive primaries used in four-colour printing.

Deboss
As emboss but recessed into the substrate.

Descender
Part of a lower case letter that extends below the baseline.

Die cut
Special shapes cut in a substrate by a steel rule.

Display type
Large and/or distinctive type intended to attract the eye. Specifically cut to be viewed from a distance.

Dot gain
Spreading and enlarging of ink dots on paper.

Down stroke
The heavy stroke in a type character.

DPI (Dots Per Inch)
The resolution of a screen image or printed page.

Drop cap
Large initial at the start of a text that drops into lines of type below.

Dummy
Provisional layout showing illustration and text positions as they will appear in the final reproduction.

Duotone
A two-colour reproduction from a monochrome original.

Em
Unit of measurement derived from width of the square body of the cast upper case M. An em equals the size of a given type i.e. the em of 10 point type is 10 points.

Emboss
A design stamped without ink or foil giving a raised surface.

En
Unit of measurement equal to half of one em.

EPS (Encapsulated PostScript)
A picture file format for storing vector or object-based artwork, and bitmaps. EPS files can be resized, distorted and colour separated but no content alteration can usually be made.

Family
Fonts sharing common design characteristics but with different sizes and weights.

Foil stamp
Foil pressed on to a substrate using heat and pressure. Also known as heat stamp, hot stamp, block print or foil emboss.

Font
The physical attributes needed to make a typeface, be it film, metal, wood or PostScript information.

Format
The size/proportions of a book or page.

Four-colour printing
Full colour printing method using colour separation and CMYK inks.

GIF (Graphic Interchange Format)
A storage format suitable for images with flat areas of colour, such as text and logos.

Golden Section
A division in the ratio 8:13 that produces harmonious proportions.

Greyscale
A tonal scale that enables a printer to check tone reproduction.

Grid
A guide or template to help obtain design consistency.

Gutter
The space that comprises the fore edge, or outer edge of a page, that is parallel to the back and the trim. The centre alleyway where two pages meet at the spine and the space between text columns are also

called the gutter.

Halftone
The simulation of a continuous tone by a pattern of dots.

Hue
A pure colour that does not include any black or white.

Imposition
The arrangement of pages in the sequence and position in which they will appear when printed before being cut, folded and trimmed.

Ink trapping
The adjustment of areas of colour, text or shapes to account for misregistration on the printing press by overlapping them.

International paper sizes (ISO)
A range of standard paper sizes.

Italic
A slanted variety of typeface often used for emphasis.

JPEG (Joint Photographic Experts Group)
A file format for storing photographic images. Contains 24-bit colour information i.e. 6.7million colours, using compression to discard image information. Suitable for images with complex pixel gradations but not for flat colour.

Justify
Formatting to space out lines of type uniformly to a fixed width.

Kerning
The removal of unwanted space between letters.

Layout
The placement of text and images to give the general appearance of a printed page.

Leading
Vertical space between lines of type measured in points.

Ligature
Tied type characters. Common ligatures are: fi, fl, ffi, ffl, and ff, and also the vowel pairs ae and oe.

Magenta
A shade of red, one of the subtractive primaries used in four-colour printing.

Majuscule
Upper case letter.

Matter
Copy to be printed.

Margin
The empty areas on a page that surround the printed matter.

Measure
The width of a block of type.

Metallic ink
A printing ink that gives a gold, silver, bronze etc. effect.

Minuscule
Lower case letter.

Moiré
A printing error where halftones appear as visible dots.

Monochrome
An image made of varying tones of one colour.

Oblique
A slanting typographic character also called solidus.

Optical character recognition
A process of scanning printed text and converting to editable matter.

Original
Any matter or image for reproduction.

Pica
Unit of measurement equal to one sixth of an inch comprising 12 points.

Pigment
Material used as the colouring agent of inks and paint.

PMS
Pantone Matching System, a colour matching system.

Point
Unit of measurement equal to 1/72 of an inch used to measure type.

Primary colours
Red, green and blue, the primary colours of light, also called additive primaries.

Process colours
The subtractive primaries: cyan, magenta, yellow and black used for full-colour reproduction.

RA paper size
Untrimmed paper sizes in the international paper size series.

Registration
Exact alignment of two or more printed images with each other on the same substrate.

RGB
Red, green and blue, the additive primaries.

Rule
A line added for emphasis.

Saddle stitch
A binding that uses a wire staple to fasten folded pages.

Sans-serif
Having no serif.

Saturation
The colour variation of the same tonal brightness from none to pure colour.

Screen angle
Relative angles of halftone screens in four-colour process reproduction to avoid moiré patterns.

Screen-printing
The direct imprinting of a design on to the surface of a substrate, usually using paint.

Script
A typeface that imitates handwriting.

Serif
A small terminal stroke that accentuates the end of the main stroke of a letter.

Spot colour or special
A specially mixed colour.

SRA paper size
Untrimmed paper sizes for bleed work in the international paper size series.

Stem
The most prominent vertical, or closest to vertical, stroke in a type character.

Stock
The paper to be printed upon.

Stress
Variation in letter stroke thicknesses.

Substrate
A surface to be printed on.

Tagged Image File Format (TIFF)
A flexible method for storing images.

Text
Written or printed matter that forms the body of a publication.

Tonal value
Image's relative tone densities.

Typeface
The letters, numbers and punctuation marks of a typeface.

Type size
The size of type, measured in points between the bottom of the descender and the top of the ascender.

Upstroke
The finer stroke of a type character.

UV coating
Coating applied to a printed substrate that is bonded and cured with ultraviolet light.

Varnish
Coating applied to a printed sheet for protection or appearance.

X-height
The height of lower-case letters such as 'x' with no ascenders or descenders.

index

Compiled by Indexing
Specialists (UK) Ltd

contacts and credits

All reasonable attempts have been made to trace, clear and credit the copyright holders of the images reproduced in this book. However, if any credits have been inadvertently omitted, the publisher will endeavour to incorporate amendments in future editions.

Lynne Elvins/Naomi Goulder

Working with ethics

The Fundamentals
of Creative Design

Ethical:
aware-
ness/
reflect-
ion/
debate

Publisher's note

The subject of ethics is not new, yet its consideration within the applied visual arts is perhaps not as prevalent as it might be. Our aim here is to help a new generation of students, educators and practitioners find a methodology for structuring their thoughts and reflections in this vital area.

AVA Publishing hopes that these **Working with ethics** pages provide a platform for consideration and a flexible method for incorporating ethical concerns in the work of educators, students and professionals. Our approach consists of four parts:

The **introduction** is intended to be an accessible snapshot of the ethical landscape, both in terms of historical development and current dominant themes.

The **framework** positions ethical consideration into four areas and poses questions about the practical implications that might occur. Marking your response to each of these questions on the scale shown will allow your reactions to be further explored by comparison.

The **case study** sets out a real project and then poses some ethical questions for further consideration. This is a focus point for a debate rather than a critical analysis so there are no predetermined right or wrong answers.

A selection of **further reading** for you to consider areas of particular interest in more detail.

Introduction

Ethics is a complex subject that interlaces the idea of responsibilities to society with a wide range of considerations relevant to the character and happiness of the individual. It concerns virtues of compassion, loyalty and strength, but also of confidence, imagination, humour and optimism. As introduced in ancient Greek philosophy, the fundamental ethical question is: *what should I do?* How we might pursue a 'good' life not only raises moral concerns about the effects of our actions on others, but also personal concerns about our own integrity.

In modern times the most important and controversial questions in ethics have been the moral ones. With growing populations and improvements in mobility and communications, it is not surprising that considerations about how to structure our lives together on the planet should come to the forefront. For visual artists and communicators, it should be no surprise that these considerations will enter into the creative process.

Some ethical considerations are already enshrined in government laws and regulations or in professional codes of conduct. For example, plagiarism and breaches of confidentiality can be punishable offences. Legislation in various nations makes it unlawful to exclude people with disabilities from accessing information or spaces. The trade of ivory as a material has been banned in many countries. In these cases, a clear line has been drawn under what is unacceptable.

But most ethical matters remain open to debate, among experts and lay-people alike, and in the end we have to make our own choices on the basis of our own guiding principles or values. Is it more ethical to work for a charity than for a commercial company? Is it unethical to create something that others find ugly or offensive?

Specific questions such as these may lead to other questions that are more abstract. For example, is it only effects on humans (and what they care about) that are important, or might effects on the natural world require attention too?

Is promoting ethical consequences justified even when it requires ethical sacrifices along the way? Must there be a single unifying theory of ethics (such as the Utilitarian thesis that the right course of action is always the one that leads to the greatest happiness of the greatest number), or might there always be many different ethical values that pull a person in various directions?

As we enter into ethical debate and engage with these dilemmas on a personal and professional level, we may change our views or change our view of others. The real test though is whether, as we reflect on these matters, we change the way we act as well as the way we think. Socrates, the 'father' of philosophy, proposed that people will naturally do 'good' if they know what is right. But this point might only lead us to yet another question: *how do we know what is right?*

You
What are your ethical beliefs?

Central to everything you do will be your attitude to people and issues around you. For some people, their ethics are an active part of the decisions they make every day as a consumer, a voter or a working professional. Others may think about ethics very little and yet this does not automatically make them unethical. Personal beliefs, lifestyle, politics, nationality, religion, gender, class or education can all influence your ethical viewpoint.

Using the scale, where would you place yourself? What do you take into account to make your decision? Compare results with your friends or colleagues.

Your client
What are your terms?

Working relationships are central to whether ethics can be embedded into a project, and your conduct on a day-to-day basis is a demonstration of your professional ethics. The decision with the biggest impact is whom you choose to work with in the first place. Cigarette companies or arms traders are often-cited examples when talking about where a line might be drawn, but rarely are real situations so extreme. At what point might you turn down a project on ethical grounds and how much does the reality of having to earn a living affect your ability to choose?

Using the scale, where would you place a project? How does this compare to your personal ethical level?

01 02 03 04 05 06 07 08 09 10

01 02 03 04 05 06 07 08 09 10

Your specifications
What are the impacts of your materials?

In relatively recent times, we are learning that many natural materials are in short supply. At the same time, we are increasingly aware that some man-made materials can have harmful, long-term effects on people or the planet. How much do you know about the materials that you use? Do you know where they come from, how far they travel and under what conditions they are obtained? When your creation is no longer needed, will it be easy and safe to recycle? Will it disappear without a trace? Are these considerations your responsibility or are they out of your hands?

Using the scale, mark how ethical your material choices are.

Your creation
What is the purpose of your work?

Between you, your colleagues and an agreed brief, what will your creation achieve? What purpose will it have in society and will it make a positive contribution? Should your work result in more than commercial success or industry awards? Might your creation help save lives, educate, protect or inspire? Form and function are two established aspects of judging a creation, but there is little consensus on the obligations of visual artists and communicators toward society, or the role they might have in solving social or environmental problems. If you want recognition for being the creator, how responsible are you for what you create and where might that responsibility end?

Using the scale, mark how ethical the purpose of your work is.

01 02 03 04 05 06 07 08 09 10

01 02 03 04 05 06 07 08 09 10

Working with ethics

One aspect of graphic design that raises an ethical dilemma is that of its relationship with the creation of printed materials and the environmental impacts of print production. For example, in the UK, it is estimated that around 5.4 billion items of addressed direct mail are sent out every year and these, along with other promotional inserts, amount to over half a million tonnes of paper annually (almost 5 per cent of the UK consumption of paper and board). Response rates to mail campaigns are known to be between 1–3 per cent, making junk mail arguably one of the least environmentally friendly forms of print communication. As well as the use of paper or board, the design decisions to use scratch-off panels, heavily coated gloss finishes, full-colour ink-intensive graphics or glues for seals or fixings make paper more difficult to recycle once it has been discarded. How much responsibility should a graphic designer have in this situation if a client has already chosen to embark on a direct mail campaign and has a format in mind? Even if designers wish to minimise the environmental impacts of print materials, what might they most usefully do?

In 1951, Leo Burnett (the famous advertising executive known for creating the Jolly Green Giant and the Marlboro Man) was hired to create a campaign for Kellogg's new cereal, Sugar Frosted Flakes (now Frosties in the UK and Frosted Flakes in the US). Tony the Tiger, designed by children's book illustrator Martin Provensen, was one of four characters selected to sell the cereal. Newt the Gnu and Elmo the Elephant never made it to the shelves and after Tony proved more popular than Katy the Kangaroo, she was dropped from packs after the first year.

Whilst the orange-and-black tiger stripes and the red kerchief have remained, Provensen's original design for Tony has changed significantly since he first appeared in 1952. Tony started out with an American football-shaped head, which later became more rounded, and his eye colour changed from green to gold. Today, his head is more angular and he sits on a predominantly blue background. Tony was initially presented as a character that walked on all fours and was no bigger than a cereal box. By the 1970s, Tony's physique had developed into a slim and muscular six-foot-tall standing figure.

Between 1952 and 1995 Kellogg's are said to have spent more than USD$1 billion promoting Frosted Flakes with Tony's image, while generating USD$5.3 billion in gross US sales. But surveys by consumer rights groups such as Which? find that over 75 per cent of people believe that using characters on packaging makes it hard for parents to say no to their children. In these surveys, Kellogg's come under specific scrutiny for Frosties, which are said to contain one third sugar and more salt than the Food Standards Agency recommends. In response, Kellogg's have said: 'We are committed to responsibly marketing our brands and communicating their intrinsic qualities so that our customers can make informed choices.'

Food campaigners claim that the use of cartoon characters is a particularly manipulative part of the problem and governments should stop them being used on less healthy children's foods. But in 2008, spokespeople for the Food and Drink Federation in the UK, said: 'We are baffled as to why Which? wants to take all

Is it more ethical to create promotional graphics for 'healthy' rather than 'unhealthy' food products?

Is it unethical to design cartoon characters to appeal to children for commercial purposes?

Would you have worked on this project, either now or in the 1950s?

I studied graphic design in Germany, and my professor emphasised the responsibility that designers and illustrators have towards the people they create things for.

Eric Carle
(illustrator)

AIGA
Design Business and Ethics
2007, AIGA

Eaton, Marcia Muelder
Aesthetics and the Good Life
1989, Associated University Press

Ellison, David
Ethics and Aesthetics in European Modernist Literature:
From the Sublime to the Uncanny
2001, Cambridge University Press

Fenner, David E W (Ed)
Ethics and the Arts:
An Anthology
1995, Garland Reference Library of Social Science

Gini, Al and Marcoux, Alexei M
Case Studies in Business Ethics
2005, Prentice Hall

McDonough, William and Braungart, Michael
Cradle to Cradle:
Remaking the Way We Make Things
2002, North Point Press

Papanek, Victor
Design for the Real World:
Making to Measure
1972, Thames & Hudson

United Nations Global Compact
The Ten Principles
www.unglobalcompact.org/AboutTheGC/TheTenPrinciples/index.html